You Are Here for a Reason

The Angel Behind Me

Celeste Gianni

Balboa Press books may be ordered through booksellers or by contacting:

Balboa Press
A Division of Hay House
1663 Liberty Drive
Bloomington, IN 47403
www.balboapress.com.au
1 (877) 407-4847

Print information available on the last page.

ISBN: 978-1-5043-1822-8 (sc)
ISBN: 978-1-5043-1823-5 (e)

Balboa Press rev. date: 07/22/2019

Contents

Introduction

Write a book, they said. You have to tell your story. Therefore, here goes. This book had to happen not by choice but because of necessity. It is what you have to do if you refuse to pay attention to forces from the other side trying to get messages to you; you need a wake-up call, not once but twice. I ignored this for years because I really didn't believe I had a story worth telling.

It is what happens when it occurs to you that random strangers are more in tune with your life and life story than you are. It is that light bulb moment, when it dawns on you how out of touch with your own existence you have become; how over time you have managed to lose not only your identity but also your voice and your whole life purpose. When several strangers stop you and refer to your multiple near-death experiences and you look at them as though they are aliens because you have never had a near-death experience, let alone multiple ones.

So why would I write a book? What could I possibly have to share? Seriously, though, jokes aside, after all, I haven't invented anything amazing or conquered mountains. What could I possibly have that is even remotely worth sharing with you—or anyone else, for that matter?

Tighten your seat belts and brace yourself for the ride, as I have no idea where I am going with this or where it will lead. I think there will be laughs, tears (mostly mine) and hopefully some self-discovery along the way. Now I am hopefully going to be that person who, when I reach the end of this project, will be able to say that this process has been cathartic, a massive exercise in healing not only my body but also my mind and spirit. Here's hoping anyway that this is where I end up.

After all, I'm nothing special, just a normal wife, mother, daughter, sister, and grandmother. What amazing stories could I possibly have that might be worth sharing with the masses? There is nothing special to see here—no mountains climbed literally, of course, no life-changing inventions saving lives in the third world. I seriously wonder how someone like me could have anything worth sharing or be of any interest to anyone else. Yes, I know I'm repeating myself, but OMG, this is only the introduction.

I would like to thank my girls, Mikaela and Ashley, for being the incredible humans that they are and so blessed to have them in my life. I have raised them to believe they can achieve anything they set their minds to. Now it is time for me to do the same, to practice what I preach.

To my husband, John, for holding me through some of my darkest, most painful moments as well as sharing all the fantastic milestones we have shared together. Thank you. I know this has been a difficult journey for us, but hopefully we can come out stronger at the other end. We married young and had to face problems and situations that no young couple should face. We worked through it as best we could at the time. We have come through it all much stronger and more united as a family.

A massive thank-you to my parents, who at the age of eighty not only became my full-time carers but also were there for my family, making sure there was a hot meal on the table for them after four months of living on takeout. If it were not for them, I would not have had the energy to research myself back to good health and be where I am today.

A big thank-you also to my annoying little brother, James, who was an absolute pain in the ass when we were kids but who was my go-to, lean-on guy and my rock every time and anytime I needed him. He only needed to see my phone number pop up on his phone, and he would be there within minutes with his drill to fix something for me. He helped me move thirty years of furniture and stuff into storage, at the darkest, most desperate time of my life. He was always there for my kids and me; I only needed to ask. I do not think he realises the enormity of what I have been through or how vital his support was during critical times. I constantly tell him how much I love him and his family, but he thinks I'm nuts. OK, OK, he *knows* I am nuts.

Also a big thank-you to three other amazing women who came into my life, in what I have now come to understand as *divine timing*:

1. To my wonderful naturopath/chiropractor and homeopath, who listened to my aches and pains and offered solutions and who kept boosting my immune system to help me function while other doctors scratched their heads and sent me home a crumpled mess, convinced there was nothing wrong with me. This nightmare went on for thirty years. If it were not for her, I am sure I would not be here now, and I would not be in the shape that I am now, living a reasonable life rather than that of a frail invalid.
2. To my best friend, Amy, my soul sister, who, while on her own spiritual journey, took time out to listen to her inner voice telling her to get me a voucher for *reconnective healing*, which was something that I knew nothing about and without which I would still be quite a few steps behind in my spiritual journey.
3. To the third and final amazing woman, the reconnective healer who reconnected me to my very own lost soul and told me everything I already knew but validated just how lost I was spiritually and put me back together.

I have come to the realization that life is a series of lessons that help us grow. Sometimes we are reluctant to allow ourselves to move through the levels or different stages because of ingrained habits. Most times this happens because of entrenched doubt and lack of confidence, usually carried through from our childhoods and even past lives without our even being aware of it. Most of all, we choose to ignore our inner voices that are always there to guide us. While working through these lessons, I also came to understand that perhaps this is why, throughout my life, I often felt as though I was outside looking in. Every time I was bombarded with something negative, I always had a sense that I was being tested.

Just think of your life this way: Do you find yourself constantly repeating the same patterns? Whether it is life-style, relationships, habits: how you react to certain people, or how you allow other people to play you time and time again, just as if you're watching a train wreck happening in front of you and you know exactly what you're about to do but you're totally powerless to stop it? You already know how it is going to end as you have been playing this game on repeat your whole life.

If you are like me, it is going to take several thunderbolts from the other side to make you pay attention and remove these self-imposed blocks. You have to lift these blocks and allow your real self to finally rise up.

This is why life is a journey at times blessed and other times dark and challenging, and sometimes we need to come up against the worst life can throw at us to really learn the lessons we need to learn and to shine at the other end.

Sometimes we get so caught up with the day-to-day, mundane stuff of life that we forget to smell the roses or really look at the beauty in the simplest and most obvious things right under our noses until that proverbial wake-up call slaps us in the face so hard that we stand up and take notice.

Chapter 1

The Early Years

I guess when you write a book, the best place to start is the beginning.

I was born in 1964 to hard-working migrant parents in a working-class suburb of Melbourne. My brother was born in 1969, and from very young ages, we were latchkey kids. I found I was constantly using my intuition to keep us safe, this was normal back then when both parents were out working. My mother was working night shift and my father day shift and there was a brief 20 minutes between my mother leaving for her night shift and my father returning where we were alone. My mother would feed and change my brother leave him in his cot and I would be entertained in front of the TV with firm instructions not to move until my father came home. I was also not to ever answer the door. My parents had hardly any family in Australia they did not have too many options.

What became evident to me early in my childhood was that I did not quite fit into my age group. Kids my age were immature, and it was always going against the grain for me to do and act as they were. What was evident very early on was a sense of knowing. I'm not sure how to explain it, but it was always there. I really did have a mind of my own and a very strong sense of knowing. I just knew things that I couldn't explain. Confused? I was too.

This might explain why I avoided getting caught up in grief as other kids my age often did. I always knew how things were going to end up and avoided getting into anything otherwise known as trouble. I always had the good little voice in my head saying, "Not a good idea." Luckily for me, I suppose that more often than not I listened. This was useful during the teenage years especially, even though it made me restless in other ways. I was headstrong and not afraid to stand alone, and I have always had very strong opinions. To be very honest, I was not the perfect child, but I did not get up to nearly as much mischief as my friends did.

I also knew on sight which people I liked or disliked, and I was always right.

Now when you are fifteen, it is more important to be one of the popular kids; however, every time one of my friends came to me for advice, things just panned out exactly as I had predicted. If they didn't heed my warning or advice, it was always to their detriment.

I was more like everyone's "Dear Abby," always being pinned down for advice and drained by the experience. Seriously, I should have started charging for my time. Often I felt more like a shrink than a kid.

Part of this knowing was I always felt I was going to write a book. I never wanted to write a book, but I knew I was going to, a book about my experiences and hopefully an inspiration to anyone out there who may be struggling with chronic illness, losing hope, and ready to throw in the towel. That's a place I know only too well and have visited often.

Now let's be straight here: I'm not thinking bestseller or literary prize award of any sort. See now, here is the ingrained doubt and lack of confidence. We have not even met, and I am telling you how my book is not really going anywhere. Does this sound familiar?

This is a story about my journey, as crazy and unbelievable as that journey may sound. Who knows? It may help someone else out there who shared similar experiences or had questions as I did. In addition, it will remain as a record of my journey for my kids and grandkids in case my spiritual gift or autoimmune issues happen to be handed down to them someday. After all, who knows how all this ties into the greater scheme of things?

My younger daughter has also had visions, and the older one has had prophetic dreams; it looks like my girls also have a gift just begging to be developed.

After an MRI several years ago, I was diagnosed with white matter on my brain. This was already affecting memory; I often was losing my words and my train of thought, which in a way added to the urgency of putting my experiences and story on paper. This might also explain why this project has taken nearly four years to get to print, not because of the size of the book but because of the time constraints, my health issues initially, and then the time dedicated to caring for my aging parents.

Maybe in writing it, by the time I get to the end of this story, I will understand my life's purpose.

My knowing that I was going to write a book always had me sitting in front of big windows, gazing over hills and trees, while typing away furiously. Funnily enough, I look up and realise I'm sitting in front of large windows doing just that. This has always been on my radar, even when I have spent a lifetime dismissing the idea and denying it. It was always in the "maybe-one-day" basket. However, as I said before, I didn't think I had a story, let alone one worth sharing.

Now I have finally decided to give in and start honouring myself for a change. I will start being true to myself and not be who everyone else thinks I should be.

I believe that because I have not done that in a very long time, my grief or lack of nurturing of my soul and the real me have manifested in the form of illness, even at times multiple illnesses. I will share more about that later.

Ghosts

I cannot say that as a child, I had ever seen a ghost, and even if I had, I would not have been aware of the difference. The only ghost-related story from my childhood is that I told my mother that I remembered the man in a photo we were looking at. He was playing with me when I was a baby. I remember telling my mother that he was a really nice man and that he always made me laugh. I also remembered playing on the bed in the photo with him. My mother told me that that was impossible because he died when I was still an infant.

A drunk driver tragically knocked down this man, as he was crossing the road outside his home and he later died in hospital. He was my uncle and I was merely months old when he died.

Shortly after his death, my parents moved into his home to help my auntie through her grief and help her with her young daughter. I was often put on the bed, and various people in the house would play with me. Funnily enough, I don't remember any of the others playing with me, and I should have been far too young to remember the man in the photo.

We are always told that children up to the age of six or ten (depending on whom you speak to) see spirits, and I've often observed my granddaughter cooing, giggling, and chatting while alone in her room as if she has company. At the same time, on the baby monitor I can see orbs flying around her room. Then I talk into the monitor and ask the spirits to let her sleep, as she is overdue for a nap, and mysteriously the orbs vanish.

Chapter 2

Near-Death Experiences

Near-death experiences are events when the average person has one freaky story to tell in his or her lifetime. Well, near-death experiences have plagued me my whole life. There have been so many that I have a tendency to forget some or play them down. Some are dramatic, and some are not overly dramatic but serious nevertheless.

Most of my friends don't even know this about me because I never really thought it was worth discussing until now. Much of this book is also news to my husband. My story is stuff that happened to me and I have never dwelt on any of it. Somewhere in there lies a story of its very own. However, more recently, I have been thinking that collectively all this needs to be connected for some other purpose, hence the necessity of sharing this story. I feel that over the years I have somehow lost not only my identity but also my life purpose.

Don't get me wrong: it happens. It's called life. At some stage, some things take priority, and others are placed on the backburner. Along that, great life journey that we are talking about, I found that I was getting sick, developing strange and unexplainable illnesses that had doctors scratching their heads. Blood test results came back saying this or that was off, but doctors did not know what to do about it. It was a very frustrating time. I had young children and a busy life; I didn't have time to be sick or just off, as the symptoms were not obvious on the outside. Early on in our marriage, in fact, shortly after our wedding, my

Erythrocyte Sedimentation Rate reading for about twelve months was around 300 to 400, and my doctors had no explanation for it.

The years were passing, and my health just kept deteriorating. Then strange things started happening, such as random people who didn't know me stopping me in the street and feeling compelled to pass on a message from the other side. Well, at some point, you have to stop and listen. This has happened to me quite a few times. On two occasions, these incidences happened years apart and came from two psychics who were strangers to me. How I wish now that I had stopped them and grabbed a phone number for a reading. I was dumbfounded and in a state of shock both times. Besides, I had never given psychics much thought, and I knew very little about them at that point.

The first time it happened, I was walking down the street, and it was so unexpected and surreal that I was asking myself if it had really happened. The lady started to tell me that all week she'd been getting messages from her guides telling her of my multiple near-death experiences and how hard my guides had been working to keep me here and that I still had work here to do. She'd had no idea who the message was for until that very moment when she saw me in the street. Up until that moment, I had not even thought of my experiences as near-death Experiences. In fact, I nearly started arguing with her that the message must be for someone else. To me a near-death experience would have been me flat lining on an operating table and watching while floating up around the ceiling, the doctors working on saving my life. At that time, that was my interpretation of an NDE. I had no idea what to do with this information, so I just dismissed it and convinced myself that she had gotten it wrong and her message was for someone else.

The second time, I was approached in the ladies' room after a movie, and a lady told me she had a message from her guides to pass on to me. I can't remember it word for word, but again it was along the same lines. Yet again, I was left dumbfounded. On both occasions, it was so random and while I was out doing my normal activities, and it totally caught me off guard.

Also around both of these times, I was at a very low point with my health, at times questioning whether I really wanted to continue in my current state of ill health and whether life was worth living. So it was a validation and an intervention from guides to remind me that my life was given to me for a reason and I still had work here to do. I was needed.

When the second woman approached me with her message from the other side, I think she sensed the fact that I was about to disregard everything that she had just told me. On the other hand, maybe she noticed the eye-roll, where I started looking around for the hidden candid camera, wondering why all these weirdos seemed to be drawn to me, I felt as though I was a magnet for them. Her message then got more frantic, to the point where she grabbed me by the shoulders and looked me in the eyes, pleading that I had to listen this time.

At this point, a penny dropped. Firstly, how did she know that this had happened to me before? Secondly, she also mentioned near-death experiences. While again walking away, once again prepared to push the experience out of my mind and ignore it as I had done previously, the desperation in her voice rather got me thinking. What if there was truth to what these women tried to tell me? What was this work they'd both said I had to do here? Why didn't they just tell me what I was meant to do instead of talking to me in riddles?

When I got home that night, her final words, "You have to listen this time," and her obvious distress got me thinking and looking back at my life, wondering about what if any of my life experiences might actually have been missed near-death experiences. I pulled out pen and paper and started writing down car accidents. There were like four: one where the car nearly rolled over and another one where my car door flew open and I was half hanging out of the car. There was also an allergic reaction or an overdose prescribed by a doctor that caused me to go into a coma (at home). By the time. I was done there were like twelve instances that could have been considered near-death experiences. Yes, you heard: at least twelve times that I could have potentially died.

I do not consider myself exceptionally bright at times, but on the other hand, I am not stupid either, but chronic illness wears you down and demolishes what remains of your spirit. Emotionally, it tears you to shreds. I have always had a spiritual connection with those I love, but then some call that *instinct*, just like when a parent knows that if, the children are very quiet in the other room; they are definitely up to some kind of mischief.

Well, my bond with my girls is enormous, and only in the past five years or so, it occurred to us that we are all three empaths.

How did this come about? This is the "I-can-be-a-bit-thick" part. It took us years to catch on to the fact that if one of us woke up in the morning with a headache, the other two would have headaches also. If one of us had pins and needles in the right leg, so did the other two. No big deal you say? Well, it is when you do not know which one needs to take a headache tablet when all three of us wake up with a smashing headache, so that we can all get on with our day. Throw another seven or eight other autoimmune diseases on top of that, and enjoy your day—good luck. Oh, let us not even touch on the time of the month shenanigans between three women in one house. That is right—my poor husband. No wonder he spent so much time at the office.

I have also stormed into their bedrooms and say, "What?" because in my head I can hear them calling me impatiently, only to be told, "I was just about to call for you." I also did that to my husband when we were newlyweds. I felt as though I had heard him calling me five or six times when he was thinking of calling me but had not actually uttered a word yet. So let us add *mind reader* to my list of talents. This has happened too many times to mention.

On Melbourne Cup day 2014, after going to the TAB to collect my winnings from a box trifecta, I looked at my youngest and said, "What did you say? You want a Panadol?" to which her reply was "I've wanted a Panadol all day, but I didn't say anything." Again, I heard her loud and clear. She hadn't even mentioned her splitting headache.

If you are wondering how the numbers to that horse race came to me, it was after a meditation. My win was $3,600, and one week later, my car's engine spluttered and died. Yes, you guessed it—$3,530 to replace it. Now if this wasn't a direct gift at the time from above, I don't know what would have been. That is also, what is often referred to as "easy comes, easy goes." Three years later, Ashley wrote off that very same car while John and I were on holiday in Bali. Luckily, she was not hurt, and that was all that mattered.

Once I put pen to paper, thinking about my near-death experiences, I realised my near-death experiences pretty much started straight after I was born. During a bath when I was a few weeks old, my mother noticed a cyst on my upper leg. Like all new mums, she totally freaked out and rushed me to the ED. She was told I was lucky they'd gotten to it before it reached the bone marrow, as this definitely would have landed me in a wheelchair. That was miracle number one. Miracle number two was that I walked at nine months, even though I was a very chubby baby. I was lucky to have ever have walked at all. Doctors repeatedly told my parents how lucky I was, that it had been noticed and treated early. Was this the beginning of spiritual intervention or just a fluke?

As a toddler, I was constantly ill, always suffering with tonsillitis. I was at the doctor's surgery more often than not. At the age of five, I had my tonsils removed. My health improved for a short while. That was probably the only straight-forward, drama-free procedure that I had ever undergone in my life, so I thought I would mention it.

When I was about eight years old, my dad bought his first car. Now, as a migrant, that was huge. He got his driver's license, and it made life for the family so much easier. As kids, we enjoyed many wonderful day trips around Victoria, because up until that moment, I still remember our trips to the supermarket were always made on a bike with a basket attached to the back of the bike and me in front of him on the handlebars. Otherwise, we went everywhere by taxi or catching trains or trams to get anywhere.

My life was blessed like that, I had many amazing memories that I will never forget and cherish always. Our parents were hard-working and sacrificed so much to make our childhoods safe and blessed.

On one such day trip in the car, I remember we were on our way to visit friends on a farm in Timboon.

While on the freeway, somewhere between Colac and Geelong, my father swerved to miss a huge piece of wood on the road and lost control of the car. I was thrown around the back seat like a rag doll, smashing my head several times on the side window.

The car came close to rolling over several times but never did. (This was obviously before seat belt laws came to be.) The car had been travelling at high speed. The fact that none of us were hurt or more significant damage was done to the car was in itself a miracle. That was miracle number three.

Shortly after this, I began experiencing allergies to nylon, wool, and lace. My skin would break out in hives; the itching was unbearable. By the time I was ten, again I found myself going back and forth to the doctor for treatment. This one particular time, the doctor may have prescribed an adult dose or perhaps I had an allergic reaction not sure which, but the drug reacted very badly with me. I remember waking up in the morning and telling my mother that I wasn't feeling well. Now this was a common ploy with me around that time, to get time off from school. I said I was a good kid growing up; I did not say I was perfect.

So naturally my mother tried to call my bluff and insisted that I go to school. I tried to fight her not to take the morning dose of my medication, but yet again she insisted.

All I remember after taking the tablet was feeling sick in the stomach, then violently vomiting bile into the bathtub. After that, all I remember waking up in my bed three days later with the family doctor at my bedside in my home adjusting an intravenous drip. Miracle number four, I was lucky I had vomited before going under; it was like a spontaneous stomach flush. I am not sure exactly what happened or why, but I am grateful to still be here.

Everyone else was relieved, while I just thought that was the best sleep I had ever had in my life. It literally was just like coming out of a general anaesthetic. I also believe that this may have contributed to the damage my liver has sustained and in part related to some of the issues I have now.

In 1976, my family and I were fortunate enough to go to Greece on a holiday; I will try to keep it short. Who am I kidding? I'm Greek. We cannot keep anything short. While there, I had food poisoning three times in three months.

After severe dehydration and vomiting, I was rushed to hospital. My parents were not aware of the changes to the health system in Greece during their years of absence. The changes being that it did not matter whether you were on your deathbed. You would not be seeing a doctor until you offered an envelope with a monetary gift. To say we were not used to this form of health care is an understatement of mammoth proportions.

Some stranger took pity on this poor family with the sick child writhing on the floor, looking grey and moaning during a five-hour wait, to bring us up to speed. To this day, I am still not sure if the bright light I was seeing that day was in the hospital or outside the pearly gates. That obviously was miracle number five. I was eleven years old at that time. After finally getting the health care I needed, I began to slowly recover over the next week. I came very close to coming back to Australia in a box, because of something as basic as food poisoning and dehydration due to lack of medical care. I was eleven years old.

I am not too sure on the year of this one; I know I was a teenager between the ages of thirteen and fifteen. Like all good Greek migrants back then, at least one of your friends or relatives owned and ran a milk bar or a fish-and-chip shop. The milk bar was the 7-Eleven of the 1950s to 1970s before supermarkets killed them off in droves.

Back then in the 1970s, my beautiful godfather, Costa, was an owner operator of such an establishment in Burnley, Richmond, and an inner suburb of Melbourne. As was common, my family would visit on weekends. This was such a treat for me because it was my first venture into retail. He would let me serve customers, make milkshakes, and best of all, use the cash register and give back change. Laugh if you will, but for me, it was the highlight of my week. It was like playing shops for real. It was so much fun. To be totally honest, I wasn't very good at it because I was too shy.

On one particular visit while I was hanging around in front of the counter rather than behind it, I could hear the screams of a woman coming closer as she rushed into the store, screaming a blood-curdling scream. She charged through the doorway to the area behind the counter and then straight into the dwelling at the back. By the time we knew what was happening, a young man drunk or drug affected, or both, also ran in screaming, "Where's the bitch!" It was obvious that he wanted to hurt her. He was in his late twenties and very, very angry.

We found out later that he had smashed a beer bottle earlier and chased her around the house with it, wanting to kill her with it. He had also threatened their two-month-old baby earlier. This is where it got nasty. He grabbed me by my clothes with one hand and yanked on the hair on the back of my head with his other hand and wanted to trade. By this time, my family inside the dwelling had called the police, and because he did not have a weapon at the time, the police stormed the shop and arrested him quite quickly. Talk about being at the wrong place at the wrong time. It was all over in seconds.

I might have been young, but that day, I realised your life can change on a dime. It was not lost on me how different things could have worked out. What if he had had the broken bottle? What if he had had a knife? The story could have had a very different ending. I was also thankful that the police just happened to be close by and got there within minutes. To this day, if I hear raised aggressive voices, I can't help but tense up with a bit of flashback going on. I guess again someone was looking out for me. That was miracle number six. Was that yet another intervention from above just to keep me safe? Was that a near-death experience that I had totally missed or ignored yet again?

Another close call in the car was again with my dad. This time I was a passenger in the back seat behind the driver when my door got T-boned by a car that had pulled up to the left side of the road and decided to turn into a street on the right, at the precise moment my father tried to pass him.

My father tried to take evasive action in an attempt to avoid a collision, by climbing the kerb and narrowly missing a street sign, but it did not work. The car hit my rear passenger door, throwing it open. Luckily I had my seat belt on (thank god for seat belt laws), and as I was leaning half out of the car, I was watching the road about a foot and a half away from my face, and all while clinging for dear life to my seat belt.

I don't know that that was a miracle, but had I not been wearing a seat belt, my injuries would have been significant. My face would have been smeared all over the road surface, and more than likely I would have ended up under the rear wheel of the car. As the car eventually righted its self again, I was thrown back into the car and the door slammed back again. Had I not been thrown back into the car fully, I could have had major head injuries or, worse, been decapitated, being hit by a car door with such force. Again, were all of these incidents meant to be potentially fatal without intervention from above? I had never ever given them a second thought.

This one, my husband John and I will never forget. This was our *Twilight Zone* moment. It was truly and completely unbelievable and unexplainable. Now if you have any answers for me, I'm all ears. Every time my kids told people this story, they always got goose bumps and shivers, so maybe there is something more to it.

John and I were just dating back then, and we were travelling in the car on our way back to my parent's house. He had just picked me up from work in the city, and we were about three or four kilometres from my house. We were totally relationship newbies and thankfully still walking on eggshells trying to impress each other.

It was either a Thursday or a Friday, late afternoon, and as we were travelling, I heard a voice from the back seat. It was unmistakably female. It said, "Slow down." It was clear as a bell. The only problem I had was the fact that there was nobody sitting in the back seat.

Now if you were in the early stages of a relationship, it would not be a good thing to have to tell your boyfriend/girlfriend that you hear voices. Surely this would have to be relationship suicide. *What do I do? What do I say? Who was that? Do I say something? Do I ignore it?*

So I asked him to slow down as there had been many accidents on that road, and there really had been. There was a cross intersection just over a hundred meters from where we were, and back then in the early 1980s, there were no traffic lights at that intersection, hence multiple accidents.

As John took his foot slightly off the accelerator, the car began to fall back from the traffic. No sooner had I taken a breather—*Wow! That is good. I cannot believe he fell for that*—a white utility coming from the opposite direction moved over the dividing line and clipped the front headlight of the car in front of us throwing it into a 360-degree spin. As it was spinning, it totally missed our car but collected the car behind us and every other car in a fifty-meter radius in both directions. It was carnage. It was a main road, and because the cars had been travelling so close to each other, there was nowhere for them to go to avoid the huge pileup that was appearing before our eyes.

We were the only people at the scene from hell who were not injured or going off to hospital on a stretcher, we were approached by the police on scene for a statement.

The police officer at first assumed that we'd arrived on the scene after the collision, and was shocked to hear that not only were we so close behind or in front of the first few vehicles involved but also we'd seen the whole thing unfold. Not only that—John went and confronted the drunk driver of the utility, who was running around the scene trying to blame the other drivers and not taking any responsibility for crossing the road into the oncoming traffic. After all, it had been all caused by him and his actions. We could smell the alcohol on his breath from quite a distance.

The conversation with the police officer could have gone something like this: "Ah, yes, Officer, we were directly behind the first car, and, yes, in front of the third car. No, we were not injured. Nope, not a scratch on our car … What was that? How could that be? … Yes, let me explain: because I heard a voice telling us to slow down from the back seat of the car. What? You want to interview the passenger. … Sorry, Officer, not possible. It might have been a ghost or my spirit guide; I still I have no idea."

Yes, that would have made his day, not to mention my VIP pass to the funny farm. So we said we were just lucky.

Immediately after this incident, traffic lights were installed at this intersection. To this day, we don't know if there were any fatalities from the numerous casualties.

After we left the scene, we continued on our way home. By the time we walked into the house, we were still stunned and shocked by the fact that we didn't have a scratch on us.

I remember my mother took one look at us and started screaming and nearly fainted. What we had not realised was that our clothes were drenched in blood, not ours but from the injured people we had just helped load up into ambulances at the accident scene we had just left behind.

I did not tell John about the voice until a few days later. At that point, even he believed in divine intervention. He didn't even bat an eyelid. We were lucky, really lucky. To this day, I can only explain it as someone looking out for us; yet again, I was being protected by a higher source; again, a near-death experience of sorts that I had totally dismissed until a random woman orders me or pleads with me to reconnect with my life.

The impact of what actually happened that day has blown my mind ever since. The whole event was a huge shock. Then I had a bigger shock in store for me. That boyfriend actually married me. I would have thought he would run the proverbial mile. Had the shoe been on the other foot, I probably would have! This could easily be my miracle number seven.

On January 25, 1986, John and I got married. It was a wonderful day, and everything was perfect and went off like clockwork. After the reception, we decided to be different and go into the city for a drink before going back to our home. It nearly went down in the record books under the shortest-marriages-ever category. We would have crushed Kim Kardashian's first wedding statistics.

As we climbed out of the taxi, the hat I was wearing got blown off onto the road. John decided to run after it without thinking and just missed being struck by a car. The driver of the car braked hard and stopped millimetres from him. He was so lucky. Luck again was on our side, and yet again, someone was looking out for us. This was John's second near-death experience. His first was as a pre-schooler on a flight to Europe when the aeroplane experienced engine failure. That is a good excuse to be a white-knuckle flyer.

When we got married, we were still crazy, young kids, I had just turned twenty-one the month before, and he was twenty-three. Our favourite drive was to the airport to dream of the holidays we were going to have. We seriously had the travel bug, big time. Wide-eyed, wanting to see and explore the world, we would drive the thirty minutes to the airport just to watch the displays click over with the flights arriving and departing. We would enjoy watching the planes taking off and landing, and inhale the fumes just to make it feel more real—the silly things you do when you are young. Now, having said that, there is nothing wrong with dreaming. Life is not worth living without dreams and goals.

One day after one of those random drives to the airport for no other reason than to dream of future holidays, I announced that our kids and

I would be dropping him off at the airport regularly for business trips. John found this amusing and laughed hysterically. Firstly, he was and is a white-knuckle flyer, so he was convinced that that really was never going to happen.

Now, more than thirty-four years later, he has flown extensively for work. He's been to Greece at least seven or eight times, Spain, New York, Istanbul, Italy, and numerous trips to Malaysia through work, not to mention, a good thirty or so interstate trips. So yet again my prediction was right. I could clearly see myself and the kids dropping him off and waving him off at the airport. They were all work-related trips. I have not even mentioned all our personal trips. All that visualisation definitely paid off.

After a two-week honeymoon in Fiji, we were at the airport ready to go home and hoping that our flight was going to make it off the ground. We just made it off the ground, and twenty minutes later, Fiji was devastated by a cyclone. Again, we were safe and protected. All flights after ours were grounded, and the airport was closed. That was in February 1986.

On September 22, 1987, our first child, Mikaela was born. During this pregnancy and after, I realised that my senses were really active and heightened. I experienced everything from premonitions to vivid dreams to picking winning racehorses for fun and dismissing it constantly as coincidence.

Chapter 3

Premonitions

The Queen Street Massacre

The first horrifying premonition came in the form of a dream. It was the early hours of December 8, 1987. In my dream, I was on the roof of a city skyscraper. This dream was made even more terrifying by the fact that it was happening in slow motion. During the time I had this dream, I was on maternity leave from work after Mikaela's birth.

The building in my dream was a Telecom building with the old telephone symbol in a massive neon sign. In my dream, I was on the roof of this building. With me on this roof were about nine other people.

The people on the roof with me were in zombie-like states, walking to the edge and falling off one by one, a lot like the tin ducks in the shooting gallery at a fair ground where they run along the track and then flop over the side.

In my dream I was getting distressed as I tried in vain to haul each person to safety, but to no avail. I struggled and fought with all my strength, screaming, to try and pull them away from the edge. One by one, they plummeted to their deaths.

John woke me, realising I was having a nightmare. I am usually not afraid of a nightmare, because on some level, I am aware it is just a dream and that I can change the outcome. I now know that this is referred to as *lucid dreaming*, which I was not even aware that I was doing it, let alone aware that it was even a thing. However, at this time, it felt real. It was as though I was actually there; I could touch the people in front of me. I held them, trying to stop them. I looked into their eyes, but they were dead cold and had vacant stares and were not seeing me at all.

When I woke up, I was so shaken and distraught; it took me most of the day to calm my nerves, so much so that I did not even have the television on during the day. I always have the TV on in the background but not that day, I was so disturbed by my dream that I couldn't handle the noise. Around one thirty or two that afternoon, John called me to see what I thought about what was happening in the city and how freaky it all was, especially after the dream I'd had.

At this point, I knew nothing. I hadn't seen anything, no TV, no radio, nothing. I had no idea what he was referring to. Knowing how distressed I had been, he tried to make a little joke by saying I was wrong—it was not the Telecom building; it was the Australia Post office building.

That day an angry man walked into a city building shooting dead, eight people and injuring several others in the Queen Street massacre, a very dark day in the city of Melbourne. Fortunately the gunman also died on that day. Whatever demons were haunting him were put to rest before more lives were lost. Had he not died then, the death toll could have been potentially much higher.

Three days later, I had the rug pulled out from under me when I read the newspaper article explaining the building was owned by Telecom and part of it had been sublet to Australia Post. In addition, days later, I remember seeing in the newspaper the pictures of the people killed in this senseless massacre, and some of the faces seemed familiar to me, especially the picture of a young mother. It still haunts me today. The faces in the newspaper were the same faces I saw on the rooftop.

I find it frustrating in the way these messages come through. It is not as if you get an address and a phone number that you could give police in the hopes of foiling such an incident and preventing it from happening. On the other hand, is it maybe that I watch too much TV?

Another premonition, I had around the time when my beautiful baby Mikaela was not yet crawling, or even rolling, for that matter. We had just experienced a mouse plague in our area. So mice were coming into the house through the chimney and through the gaps of the walls. Our house was more than a hundred years old, so we had gaps everywhere.

I had left Mikaela on her play mat to play with her toy frame. Many of the rooms in the house had rat bait in the fireplaces. She was not walking or even crawling, so I felt safe, and I left the room to get something from the kitchen, which was at the other end of the house.

While I was in the kitchen a thought—*the baby*—popped into my head. I decided to go and check on her. I was at first shocked that she wasn't in the room that I had left her in.

My first thought was that someone was in the house. Had someone taken my baby? I ran to my bedroom, which was the next room down the corridor, and there she was. Mikaela must have rolled out of the room, down the hallway, and into my room. Her little hand was slapping in and out of the rat bait in the fireplace. Luckily, she was still much uncoordinated and had not put a handful into her mouth. She was months old and had never rolled once, let alone all the rolls in such a short time that would have gotten her down the long hallway and into another room.

Was it just good luck or angels on my side yet again? This was not my near-death experience but my baby's.

How does a baby, who had never as much as rolled over once, rolled out of one room down a hallway and into another room in such a short time? This still stumps me even now.

Walsh Street South Yarra Police Ambush

On the morning of October 12, 1988, again I had a disturbing dream. This time I was in the building I was working in at the time on Market Street, Melbourne. The basement of this building was a car park for the police, and unfortunately I hadn't been too happy with the boys in blue. Let me explain. Every morning when I walked into my building to catch the lift to my office, I came face to face with the same officers, day after day, week after week. For years, the officers never said good morning or acknowledged me. I thought this was really rude and arrogant.

Never, ever would they smile or even say hello. We walked into the same building every day. Would it kill them to say good morning once in a while or even just smile? After all, it was just manners when you come face to face with the same people every day.

In my dream, however, as I was walking out of the basement garage and onto the street to buy my lunch, something I did every day, two handsome young men in uniform with eyes twinkling with life and the most amazing, beaming smiles were walking in. Not only did they smile at me, but also they both tipped their hats in acknowledgment. Again, I felt as though we were all moving in slow motion. Wow! I was stunned and impressed. Seconds later as the police officers walked into the basement, there was a massive explosion, and I just knew that they had died.

That morning, I woke up to the devastating news that two constables in the prime of their lives had been ambushed in Walsh Street South Yarra and shot dead. I still see those beautiful smiles, and I will never forget them, both gone far too young. They were only a few years younger than I was at the time. Again in the dream, I was not given an address or any way to stop an incident like this from occurring.

Some Things Are Just Not Meant to Be

How hard is it to book a holiday you ask? Well, it depends on how many slaps in the face it takes you to understand that your guides are trying to protect you. Whether it is from tsunamis, bombings, and so on by placing constant obstacles in front of you to ensure that you and your family are spared and not find yourselves in the midst of some grand disaster? If you are anything like me, the answer is it takes many.

I had heard wonderful things about Phuket from friends over the years and had often considered it as a holiday spot, but because of one reason or another, it never came together. We kept deciding on other destinations, and Phuket was always being overlooked.

Around November 2004, we were yet again coming up with obstacles at every turn while trying to work out travel dates around John's work commitments; it just was not coming together.

We had collected travel brochures, looked at locations, and picked resorts. Try as we might, it still wasn't going to come together for us. Talk about disappointing. Again, I didn't acknowledge that there was a reason as to why my family and I were being denied a holiday to Phuket. On December 26, 2004, Thailand and surrounding countries and islands were devastated in one of the worst natural disasters I would ever in my life seen unfold. Watching the news bulletins brought to light the devastation and suffering. How lucky were we to have our lives spared because we just couldn't get it all to work.

The Boxing Day tsunami decimated several countries and claimed a massive human toll of both locals and tourists.

A couple of years later, we decided to go to Phuket as the call came for tourists to return in an attempt to get the people back to some sense of normality and to help the healing to begin.

While we were sitting at our chosen resort, I noticed that half the resort had construction going on. When we asked about this, all the staff would say was "renovation." I had a really eerie feeling that I couldn't shake. I also had a feeling that I had seen the resort before. I dismissed this thought because of the countless holiday brochures that I had mulled over for ages in the planning of our trip. I thought at first that that was why it looked familiar.

A few days into our holiday we met and spoke to other Australians who were also staying at the same resort who knew more. The reality was this resort was the main one on the news bulletins where viewers saw the wave coming in and people clinging to trees for their lives. The other Australians also showed us marks on an upper balcony that clearly indicated a water-level mark. I couldn't believe that I hadn't made the connection before.

I had been wondering why the staff working at this resort didn't speak any English. The reason for this was that the original crew all perished on that day.

The day before this realization, I was getting frustrated because I'd called housekeeping to report a blocked toilet, and a few minutes later a little Thai man who obviously didn't understand what my little tirade was about appeared at our door with a roll of toilet paper. Talk about humbling. I thought I would never judge, never sweat the small stuff in my life again, and I would appreciate every day and every moment.

On the beach of the resort were a group of local girls who offered massages, manicures, pedicures, hair braiding, and so on. The girls were entertained by Ashley who was in total awe of the thousands or so hermit crabs crawling all over the sand. Ashley had begged me for years to buy her some, but as we travelled quite a bit, we really did not need any more pets to worry about accommodating while we were away from home. At least once a day, Ashley dragged us down to the beach so she could play with the hermit crabs. There were thousands of them, and from a distance, they looked like a wave in motion.

Over the next few weeks, we got to know the girls well. They bought out three photo albums of photos of the aftermath. The images brought me down to earth with a bang so powerful that the news clips I had seen at home were nothing in comparison.

Piles of bodies, bloated and swollen, had been left by the waves anywhere and everywhere once the waves had receded, the bodies of tourists, locals, men, women and children rotting and bloated. We all started crying, the girls because some of the people in the pictures were their friends and family and me because I had never felt so useless and spoilt in all my life. They had lost their will to go on, and here I was, whining because I had a few aches and pains and a bit of discomfort. A blocked toilet was causing me such angst, totally missing the fact that I had the opportunity to tuck my loved ones into bed every night, safe and secure, surrounded by love, because a few years before my guides stepped in to prevent me and my family from making our debut in that photo album.

The realisation that the piles of bodies could have been us brought us down to earth with a thud. Isn't that a selfish thought, to be grateful that it's someone else's family in the photographs and not mine? We had angels looking out for us. Why weren't angels looking out for all the others? Who made that call and why?

I realised that while my life just continued after seeing the initial event on TV, for the people in Phuket, it was almost as though time had stood still and they had just started to breathe again and rebuild.

In 2005, my family and I were planning a return trip to Bali. We had gone in 2000, but Ashley ended up with chicken pox, so she missed out; so we had promised to take her as soon as we could. We couldn't wait to get there. While we were discussing plans and swapping and changing dates and flights, the second Bali bombing happened, and—yes, you guessed—it was at our favourite location right on the beach of Jimbaran Bay at the restaurants on the sand. It was obvious that the luck fairy had intervened yet again.

See what I meant before about so many little things that you forget them, even though they really are quite significant? We could have found ourselves at the wrong place at the wrong time on multiple occasions.

All of the above near misses have taught me not to push. If something is not coming together, don't try to force it. There just might be a higher power intervening on your behalf for your own good. Everything really does happen for a reason—corny but so true.

Chapter 4

Who Am I?

This book is more for me to acknowledge my life's journey and to make peace with my fears, and realign again with my soul and my spirituality. Yes, I am human, and, yes, I have fears, pains, and insecurities just like the next person. Just like the next person, I have to remember to breath, smell the roses, and listen to that inner voice a lot more. I have to remember that it is OK to be human and stomp my feet like a diva occasionally.

I hope that while on this journey, I will be able to heal and forgive where I need to and reconnect my spiritual side to my physical side. I am sure it is all connected. Emotions need to be acknowledged and dealt with so that I can reach a level of forgiveness and acceptance to unlock the next level of my journey, not unlike a computer game. I am told this level is called *enlightenment*. I think I have a long way to go. I hope that by the time I reach the end of this book, things will be clearer to me.

Why is this important? Well, if you have heard the saying "the buck stops here," this is what I want. What I do not want is for my girls to go through life thinking I am weak, because that I am not. If anything, yes, my rough journey has made me strong, and instead of walking out of the tunnel a crumpled mess, I am stronger than ever. I'd rather that they see me as an inspiration than a victim.

I have also come to realise how much of my parents' grief and regrets I also carried around with me. Therefore, I am sure I also unintentionally have done the same thing to my children. We know children are sponges and they pick up much more than we would like to give them credit for. They pick up the behaviours and mantras that we churn out on a daily basis, much like broken records. If you hate your body every time you look in the mirror, be careful of what comes out of your mouth, especially if little ears are around. This is baggage, and it is not only ours—it also gets unloaded onto our kids. They can see a flippant negative comment toward your partner as something serious. Every time they hear something negative, they lose their power and take on another burden by carrying our grief also.

I have only now realized how much of my father's failings and regrets I carry around with me, or my mothers' paralysed will. She was always homesick, and she missed her siblings, whom she was extremely close to. She never really felt at home here or happy with her life, for her own reasons. I do not want to do the same thing to my kids, and I realize finally that unintentionally at times I have done that exact same thing. I have realised that although my childhood for most of the time was ideal, blessed, and innocent, as I got older, I felt burdened by my parent's regrets. Also, as they aged, these regrets came to the surface more and more, to the point that you really couldn't talk about their younger years without the raw emotions and anger coming out.

As we all know, you go through life with plans. You graduate high school, go on to further education, get a job, start a family, and aim for success. Plans and direction are great, but occasionally life happens and the road you are catapulted on takes you on a completely different course altogether that you have absolutely no control over.

As I get deeper into telling this story, I realise how much I had dropped the things I actually wanted to do or achieve for me in my life—to the point of totally neglecting them. Is this why my guides felt it was important to intervene by bringing in strangers to get my attention?

Chapter 5

Premonition or Just Bloody Good Guesses

My Spiritual Journey

When I was young, I had a special connection with a higher being. Not that I understood it at the time. I just thought I had an uncanny knack for thinking about things that would happen. I also would advise people not to do something and then be proven right.

I never considered myself religious because I always blamed religions for all the problems in the world. I also told anyone who asked that I was an atheist, and I did not like priests, but they always seemed to have me on their radar. They scared me! I'm spiritual, yes, but not religious.

Still, I'm not sure that I can say that I believe in God as such, but I do believe in a higher being or energy.

The funny part is, while I was spruiking how much I did not believe, it took me years to acknowledge that all along I had a direct line or connection to the upstairs office. Not only that, but also, all along, my life was being protected time and time again, because I had work to do here on earth apparently!

While random people were stopping me in the street to give me messages from the other side about my multiple near-death experiences, which up until this point I had not even considered relevant in any way—yes, I hear you: the joke is on me. — I needed a wake-up call from the other side to realise that this did not just happen to everyone! Not one wake-up call but many. Not to mention the many other readings that I had had over the years from psychics, where the same message would pop up all the time. Even though I did not think much of psychics, I had several close friends who were the opposite and would not make a move until their psychic approved it. I would find myself tagging along for the fun of it.

The other thing that I noticed was that I was going through a type of unconscious cleansing phase. Fake and materialistic social climbers were out, while earthy, evolved, centred people were in. While I had developed illnesses that forced me into a type of isolation, I noticed a change in the quality and calibre of people around me.

The fake and very self-absorbed, negative, doom-and-gloom people who walked in and out of my life every day eventually dropped off the face of the earth. This was so refreshing. It was almost like a rebirth.

The nature of my illness became so debilitating that in 2011 my family and I had to place all our belongings into storage and to move in with my eighty-year-old parents. This was so that my parents could help my husband care for me till I died.

At the same time, I noticed a different type of person was drawn to us—genuine friends who were there for you, not for what they can get out of you or what you could do for them. This was so new and refreshing that up until that point I had not even realised this was what had been missing from my life.

Health books and references to spirituality that I needed were all coming to me one way or another. Answers and solutions to help in my recovery were coming at me from all directions. Google was my friend, and I was able to find ways to help my spirituality develop and reverse my allergies to some degree and, by doing so, make life fun again instead of fraught with fear. Information and guidance was unfolding before me, and it was like food for my soul. My research was actually getting me somewhere. As I said earlier, not too bright at times and slow on the uptake, but never mind, so long as we get there in the end. That is all that matters.

My health was turning a corner, and I felt I was getting stronger. Was it in my imagination?

Chapter 6

Living in an Old House

Living in an old house had been interesting. Living in an old house with children who are aware of spirits and a husband who doesn't want to know because the whole thing spooks him turns into a juggling act.

It was not unusual to hear taps running in the middle of the night; footsteps running on the floorboards when you know you are home alone; the clanging of crystal on the granite bench in the kitchen again when you are home alone. There was constant activity in that house the doorbell ringing when there's nobody there; the phone ringing when there's nobody on the other end; and footsteps of people running around upstairs in the house next door (the house next door is single storey with an elderly lady living there alone). We also had a ghost dog that ran around looking for our dog when she was away at the groomers. We could hear its collar and tags jiggling as it ran around the house.

On one occasion, I saw the spirit of what I thought was an old woman. I actually walked right through her. I was walking around a corner, and she caught me by surprise. She was like a fog or a mist. I remember one time, late at night, John (the nonbeliever) also caught what he thought was her reflection in our French doors. He came back into our bedroom to tell me he thought he saw an old woman; I quickly changed the subject because I didn't want to be moving house.

I also lost count of how many times I flicked a light switch, and light globes kept exploding straight out of the socket. It only ever happened to me. It even happened to me when some girlfriends and I went away for a weekend to Daylesford. We booked a cute little unit, and again I flicked a switch, and the light globe smashed into multiple pieces over my friends' heads. The girls nearly died when I said it happened to me all the time, as it had never happened to any of them, ever.

On another occasion in 1991 Mikaela (four years old at the time) informed me that she didn't have a good sleep because the ladies in the hallway with the big hooped skirts were making too much noise and they woke her with their laughing and loud talking. What does a four-year-old know about hooped skirts? We did not have any living guests staying with us at that time, so who were they? The house was well over 100 years old and was one of eight row houses, which was built for war widows. The woman who lived in ours was a widow whose son had gone off to war.

Tickling my feet while I slept meant my husband copped many kicks before I realised it wasn't him. My feet get really hot at night, so I'm forever sticking them outside the covers. My four-poster bed is far too high for our fur-ball Maltese terrier to be able to reach my feet without help, so she could not have done it.

Tax time was also another interesting time in my house—maybe the spirit was a cheeky accountant. Every time I sat down to get my papers ready for our accountant, I got a tap on the shoulder, only to turn around and find no one there in the room with me. In addition, the door on the built-in cupboard in that room was always half open. I would close it and turn around a few minutes later, and it would be half-open again. Obviously someone thought that was funny, and it was. It was not creepy; it was comforting. We knew we weren't alone.

We had fun in that house; at no stage did we feel threatened by the spirits. The dangers we had to deal with were of the living kind. However, that is probably a completely different kind of book.

Chapter 7

Illness versus Spirituality

It wasn't unusual for me to become a field project for doctors and for doctors from other hospitals to be called in. My family constantly joked that we needed Dr. Gregory House from the TV show to look at my chart. The first time this happened was in 2002.

In 2002, I had another very serious near-death experience, which landed me in hospital for three days. On this day in May 2002, I presented down at the closest hospital with what I thought was a bad sinus infection. I was wearing my sunglasses, as my eyes were sensitive to the lights.

What I hadn't realised at the time was that because of all the bruising around my eyes and the swelling across my face, the hospital staff thought I was an abused wife severely beaten up. The first thing they did was separate my husband and me in the hope that I would feel comfortable and confess to the abuse before they could call in police and other relevant services. I wish I had taken a photo so I could see what the hospital staff saw that day. Over time and because the swelling came up over a three-week period, I had forgotten how bad I must have looked.

When they started the "And what brings you here today?" speech, I took off my sunglasses to show the doctor my swollen face. Remember at the beginning of the book I said I had had many weird and difficult-to-diagnose conditions that were hard to explain or understand? This was one of them. The doctors at this hospital invited their infectious diseases team and doctors from infectious diseases departments at other hospitals to sit in while they sent me off for a CT scan. By this stage, the blood tests were back, and they knew what was wrong, but they weren't telling me.

What I forgot to tell you was that for three weeks I sat at home suffering with what I thought was a sinus infection and unfortunately not getting anywhere. I had already had a couple of visits to my general practitioner, but I was not improving. After much pain and suffering, John got so frustrated with me he threw me into the car, ordering me off to hospital.

During the CT scan, I knew it was serious because I could hear the doctors, all seniors in their field, arguing behind the screen. They were disagreeing and trying to make sense of it. Apparently, as it turns out, I had a very nasty infection, from the same family as meningococcal, which apparently kills you within forty-eight hours after your body turns purple with bruise-like patches and they start to amputate limbs in an effort to save your life. If that is not successful, you die. It was that simple.

Doctor after doctor came into my room and asked the same questions as the last guy. At that point, I hadn't been told what they'd found in the blood tests after answering the same questions in one thousand different ways, and I'd had enough. I was sore and sorry—sorry I had gone into hospital to be asked stupid question after stupid question at this point I was over it.

By this stage as any frustrated patient would do, I threw my hands up and said I had had enough. I had been connected up to an IV of antibiotics! I started yelling at the last schmuck they sent in that I couldn't understand why I was being asked these stupid questions and that nobody was telling me what was wrong. He then sat on the chair next to me and started to explain what they'd found and why they were so baffled as to how and why I was still alive after three weeks of battling this type of bacteria on my own and surviving.

He also suggested that I purchase a lottery ticket because I really was extremely lucky not only to still be alive but also to still have all my limbs attached.

You might think of this as an NDE, but I never did. Here I had been given another chance at life, and the whole thing had totally been lost on me. I had totally dismissed the fact that I had cheated death once again, not only dismissing it but also not even registering it.

Therefore, you see, this is why I have lost much faith in the medical establishment. Do not get me wrong: I have much respect for what they do to put you back together after a car accident or after open-heart surgery or vital brain surgery. However, what should have been a ground breaking medical discovery got no mention in any newspaper I saw.

So why was I still alive after three weeks of sheer agony? The story went like this—vitamins. Just a few weeks before, I had decided to put myself on a major detox cleansing regime with vitamins, minerals, and antioxidants. This is apparently what saved my life and allowed me to fight the bug on my own. By taking this course of action, I had given my body the ammunition to fight the battle and keep me alive.

After one day on IV antibiotics, the swelling went down by 50 per cent. After another two days, it was nearly back to normal. The doctors were shocked by how quickly I was responding to the antibiotics, as this bacteria is generally resistant to them.

After three days on an intravenous drip with high doses of antibiotics, I went home with two weeks of heavy-duty antibiotics and a follow-up appointment. This normally would be a minimum two-month admission to hospital. Three days was unheard of.

After this experience, John and I decided to take the family to Europe. It was something we had always wanted to do, but we made excuses for spending the money on other things. I thought of the money we would have spent on my funeral and decided to turn it into a positive experience; after all, life is for living and making memories. Time suddenly became more precious to us.

Now, because over the years I got nowhere with doctors, they decided I was either a drama queen or hypochondriac within the first two seconds of my walking into a room, obviously because of how I was coming across because of my desperation for answers. I had no other choice but to research and try alternative treatments in the hope that I could give myself some quality of life. My health had started to deteriorate around the age of twenty-one. From there, the only thing that showed on a blood test would be an elevated ESR of 300-plus.

Years of fighting an ongoing war just to function on a daily basis sucks the life out of you and breaks your spirit. I had years of telling my GP that I wasn't well, only to have FBE bloods come back all clear and sent home none the wiser, even though desperately unwell.

Now stay with me here our life experience moulds us into the person that we become. Yes, I married young and found myself thrust into the world of adulthood—a kid, a mortgage, a full-time job, and my new reality and responsibilities.

"You're a big girl now, and you have bills to pay" became my mantra. During this time, it became all about my family and my home. I seemed to fall down a big hole and disappear. Sick or not, I had people depending on me, and like it or not, I had to keep going.

Somewhere between 1986 and 2010, I had totally lost me. This is where the "I hear you, sister" is ringing in my ears! What Mum or Dad doesn't feel this to some degree? I am not unique. I think that most of us lose a part of, if not most of, ourselves when we become parents. Once you have children, it is no longer about your needs. You usually come last.

My duty was to be the best wife and mother I could be. My family was and is everything to me. I worked long hours at work to come home to a husband and a child, and then I would start my second job, as all working parents do. There was never any time for me. Spirituality fell by the wayside, forgotten about or entirely dismissed. You tell me how many of us can say we have a perfect work/life balance in this day and age, let alone throwing a family into the mix.

What became evident was that I was becoming chronically ill with strange, difficult-to-diagnose illnesses. For close to thirty years, I'd developed bad migraines, so bad, in fact, that towards the end of 2010 I was so depleted of strength and spirit that I did contemplate taking my own life several times, though not for long. You wonder whether living like that is worth it. You can't possibly understand this unless you've walked in my shoes.

The thought of leaving my kids behind to deal with it, especially after having witnessed the grief of a friend and her siblings struggle with memories of their mother's suicide—there was no way that I was going to let that happen. I wasn't going to leave them with an image of their mother being weak and defeated.

Also, my memory of a neighbour in my old street when I was young; I'll never forget her blood-curdling screams when she found her eighteen-year-old daughter dead with her head in the oven and the gas turned on. Upon hearing her screams, my father was the one who ran to her aid and pulled her daughter out. Unfortunately it was too late to help her. We had to watch the mother go through years of psychiatric treatment trying to come to terms with the suicide of her only child. It was heartbreaking.

For years, I desperately visited doctors and begged for help. Most of the time, I was looked at as though I was a hypochondriac. The first thing they would do would be to request a Full Blood Evaluation blood test, and then they told me that everything was fine and that I was a picture of health. They dismissed my chronic migraines as "just migraines" and completely disregarded the list of symptoms I brought in with me. Then again, if you visit the doctor with a *list*, then of course, you are a hypochondriac. I chose to put together a list only because I forgot once I was there, and I did not want to waste time. I was desperate for answers.

I was on my own, and nobody was taking me seriously. By 2013, I had developed so many allergies, and I was starting to withdraw from the world. As if not all my other symptoms were complicating my life enough, food and meeting friends for a dinner became logistical nightmares and fell into the too-hard basket, so why bother?

How do you go to someone's house for dinner and, before you eat anything, ask to raid their refrigerator and pantry to read all the ingredients in products that they used to make sure they were safe to eat? It was easier to just stay home.

Luckily after the birth of Ashley in 1996, I was catapulted into a world of discovery, thanks to some food intolerances and sensitivities she had. Fortunately for me, in Ashley's kindergarten group, I met a mum who opened up the world of chemicals, colours, and preservatives in our foods and homes that became instrumental in working out my severe allergy to preservative 220. During this time, I did a lot of research and learned so much on the way. This mum also recommended a wonderful naturopath who, for the past nineteen years, has helped me to function and continue to live a relatively normal life.

In 2010, I felt that enough was enough. After an overseas trip, I bought back with me a massive migraine that lasted four weeks and drove me to distraction and desperation. I just couldn't shake it. At this point, I decided to be referred to an ear, nose, and throat specialist. I had never been more desperate in my life. At this point, just functioning wasn't enough. I needed a name for what was wrong with me. I wanted to know it was not in my imagination, and if it had a name, I was hoping that I could cure it. After six days in hospital and collaboration between two Melbourne hospitals, I had a name for my illness. Unfortunately, or fortunately, depending on how you want to look at it, it wasn't imaginary. This was my second major *House* moment.

Up to this point, every admission to hospital, they treated me with Panadeine Forte and sent me home dismissively, with an order to take two Panadol and go to bed. Now, with this miraculous diagnosis, when I went to hospital, they treated my migraine with morphine and actually treated me as if I had a serious illness, and it would be me asking to go home while they kept insisting that I stay another day.

When the hospital staff at the private hospital I was a regular at would see me walk in to their ED or wheeled in by ambulance, the joke was that I was back for their famous cocktail. They were referring to the medications that would go into the intravenous drip. This also included an amnesiac drug to help me forget the pain and trauma. Finally I was being heard instead of being dismissed. Prior to the diagnosis, all I was given was a "suck-it-up-princess."

I also told my neurologist that, every time I had one of the shocking migraines, I believed that it left me with cognitive decline. He told me he didn't think so, but this was later confirmed with an MRI. There was significant evidence of the disease and the vascular damage it had caused in my brain as well as white matter, more than what would be expected for someone in my age group.

I have also realised I am extremely well in tune with my body; I know instinctively when something is malfunctioning.

When I went back to my local doctor after my diagnosis, she started crying while reading the report from the hospital. My local doctor had often told me that I was being rather melodramatic, the way I carried on about a headache, and now here she was sitting before me with tears in her eyes. She was not much help for thirty years, calling me melodramatic and over the top. I have a very high pain threshold. If I say I am in pain, then it must be bad.

After all, I did have a "godawful disease" (these were the words of my specialist). The name of this illness is Wegener's granulomatosis, which destroys the small blood vessels in your body, and I have it in my brain. This diagnoses then opened the floodgates. After my diagnoses with one autoimmune disease, eventually I was diagnosed with eight or nine at one point.

I had everything from hereditary angioedema, lupus anticoagulant, ulcerative colitis, autoimmune hepatitis (which caused multiple DVTs and superficial blood clots), Churg-Strauss syndrome-vitiligo-chronic-esophagitis and lupus just to name a few.

The only thing that troubles me today is the liver is still not down to normal, but it is getting there, with occasional flare-ups. In addition, the colitis also flares up from time to time, and my liver possibly causes the blood clots. Not bad for a list of imaginary diseases.

Unfortunately, as I have said before, autoimmune diseases are internal, and you have no visible symptoms to show for it, so people do not take you seriously. At some of my most miserable times, I had people telling me how great I looked, even though I may have felt like I'd died inside, my muscles and joints were killing me, and I was aching all over.

Also, because of the pain, sleep didn't come easy, as it was difficult to find a comfortable sleeping position. It was a bit like being permanently heavily pregnant. Sleep, as we all know, is a vital part of healing the body, and if you don't get any night after night, your body is exhausted, and so is your mind.

If both my shoulders had the muscles torn from the bone and were in the process of healing, you wouldn't know that by looking at me; that I haven't been able to brush my hair for four weeks; and that my kids or my husband have had to do it for me. Not to mention getting dressed, trying to make a bed, or hanging out washing. Everyday tasks were near impossible to complete. What would have taken minutes, like making a bed, would take at least half an hour, and then require a rest upon completion. That was just one of the regular aches that plagued me. Have you ever tried to do up small buttons on a shirt or lift your arms up to tie up your hair with a torn muscle or torn muscles in both arms.

Every day was a lucky dip; you just never knew what was going to plague you from one day to the next, whether it was torn muscles; breathing issues; clicking hips, knees, or both; inflammation of the joints; or the mother of all migraines. They made it nearly impossible to get on with life.

Now, back to the migraine, let me try to describe why this migraine felt so horrific. I could feel my brain pulsating. Squeeze your head hard until it hurts and release. Stick your head in a vice and keep tightening it and then get someone to hit you repeatedly with a block of concrete. Repeat this process continuously for about five hours; it felt like my brain was dehydrating and a lead ball was banging around from one side of my skull to another continuously. It is not an exaggeration; it is exactly what it felt like. I could feel nearly every vein and artery swelling and pulsating to the point of bursting.

When occasionally I did feel a vein burst, I could then feel the warm blood run down the inside of my skull. This would also bring on the hours of vomiting, which would then bring on dehydration, which in turn required a hospital admission every time. When describing this to my GP, she called me a drama queen. Then I got the "take-two-aspirin-close-the-drapes-and-sleep-it-off" speech. Sorry, Doc, but this wasn't helpful.

The ongoing migraine was only one of the cherished gifts that Wegener's would bless me with. Failing lungs caused me, after a walk to the letterbox, to sound as if I had just come back from a ten-kilometre run. Not to mention walking up my steep staircase in my home to do my housework. I always had to rest when I got to the top and do my Darth Vader impersonation.

Ringing ears or muffled hearing might explain why I could never hear people in the psychic world talking clearly and many other random symptoms that would go around like a conveyor belt, just not knowing what was going to pop up next. Planning your day is hard enough, let alone trying to decide whether you would be OK to book your car in for a service the following week or book the kids in for dental check-ups or the hundred other things that you need to do as a parent.

As I said earlier, I am not a victim, or defenceless; if anything, I am a bloody hero. I am now in control of my own life because I took back my power and my healing.

The second rheumatology specialist told me that I would probably be dead in twelve months or five years, depending on how long the drugs used to treat this disease took to kill off my major organs one by one because of their toxicity. The medication that was being offered to me at the time usually affects kidneys and lungs, then heart, eyes, ears, brain, blah, blah, blah. That is if I did not get cancer first because that was a possible side effect from one of the medications they were recommending that I take.

When I was sent to this second rheumatologist, I was prepared. After all, I had been sick for thirty years. I knew my symptoms well, so I went in with a list of symptoms, thinking I was being helpful. He took the list off me and stuck it in my file; and he never bothered to read it. For the next eighteen months, I was told there was no cure for this godawful disease; it just needed to be monitored and managed. I went back every three months or so for a review.

On my final visit after discussing several aches and pains and looking for suggestions, he asked me to let him know when I start to get pain in my upper arms. At this point, I was so close to doing the Linda Blair head spin, but instead, I kept my cool and asked him if he had a note from me on file with a list of symptoms and if he could possibly read what was on it. Keeping in mind that this list was given to him on my first visit eighteen months prior, guess what the first symptom was? At this point, I felt so alone. I realised he was not listening, and I was wasting my time and money pinning my hopes on this man helping me. I also realised that if I put my life in the hands of these people, I wasn't going to be around to watch Ashley finish high school. This specialist was the best in his field, but his bedside manner and people skills were non-existent. His arrogance was unbearable. I knew I was going to die if I put my life in this man's hands. He didn't even see me as human, just a dollar sign. This became obvious with his billing methods.

I decided early on, much to my family's disappointment that I was not going to take the medication on offer. If I was going to live for one year or five years, I wanted quality of life, not being hooked up to chemotherapy drips spending my final months with my head in a toilet, throwing my guts up. It was not for me, not an option.

At this point, I decided to take my power back. It was my life and my right to live it as I chose. I had Google on my side, every doctor's worst nightmare. Am I bitter? Yes and no, to some degree. There is nothing worse than not being taken seriously, or being much ridiculed when you say that you demand to be permitted to decide which treatment you wish to undergo. It was, after all, my body and my life. This road that I chose was the right one for me. I have no regrets about this decision.

Armed with Google and a positive attitude, I decided I was going to take control of my health. Now do not forget that for thirty years, because nobody was taking me seriously, I had no choice but to seek alternative therapies and treatments and learn as much as I could about my condition and my health. This process allowed me to get on with life, and when I got careless or lazy and stopped looking after myself, my health would plummet yet again.

When I was first diagnosed and sent to a rheumatologist who was going to manage my condition, because there really is not a cure, so it was to be a long-term relationship my first question to him was "Can I treat this naturally?" To which, his obvious answer was no. Hello! Didn't he read my file? I am Sagittarian female, stubborn as a mule, and Greek. Seriously, he had no hope. A few years ago, I was told my Wegener's granulomatosis was in remission, and, yes, I did nothing more than take vitamins. I was put onto a high-potency, good-quality, super immune booster and multivitamin, essentially for women, which I took diligently for several years thanks to my wonderful naturopath, who took the time to see me as a human being.

Now I have had a type of epiphany; I know how to manage my health, acknowledge myself, honour myself, respect myself, and watch the diseases fall away. It seemed like the more I talked to people about all this, the more my health seemed to improve. I had a refrigerator loaded with allergy drops, more than $3,000 worth of them, that I no longer needed.

I realised that while trying to decalcify my pineal gland because my visions had stopped, I actually reversed my allergies and sensitivities. Now what would that be worth to a drug company? But then again, why would a pharmaceutical company be interested in reversing allergies when antihistamines are probably their best sellers.

Every time I got into an aeroplane, I would end up sick and in hospital upon my return. The last five times I travelled overseas, I had no such problem. On one trip, I was standing on the tarmac boarding the plane with the engines blowing fumes in my face. I didn't get a migraine, and that's where I started asking myself what had I done differently? When before petrochemicals, bus fumes, lawnmowers, and car exhausts would knock me out for days on end, here I was, standing behind a jumbo jet with engines blowing directly into my face and feeling fine, no sign of a migraine.

For a long time, I have believed that anything autoimmune is more to do with an emotional element, as well as a vitamin and mineral deficiency, than anything physical is. Now you are perfectly within your rights to disagree with me, and that is fine. After all, this is based on my opinion, experience, and nothing more. Do not get me wrong: autoimmune diseases can kill you; it is not trivial by any means. However, when looking to cure an autoimmune disease, you should also consider healing the spirit of guilt or regret by getting to the root of the pain, grief, or regret and eliminating stress, and not just focus on the medicinal side of treatment. Sometimes it is far too easy to sweep something under the carpet than to bring it out into the open and discuss with family if it is just going to stir up negative feelings. So you just bury your emotions deeper and hope that it will go away. Healing of the spirit is just as important as healing of the body.

If you think burying it is going to make it go away, here is the heads-up: it does not. Think of the problem that started this feeling as a brick. After a few years and a few more bricks, you find yourself unable to breathe under this weight because you have accumulated enough bricks to build a house. Although I was busy working and playing mum and nurturing everyone else, I was forgetting me!

Illness led me to change my diet and use meditation instead of medication to deal with pain and help me with more comfortable sleep. YouTube is free. I started playing sleep meditation videos while wearing headphones to improve my sleep, therefore not needing to resort to sleeping tablets.

Did I also mention being on my spiritual journey and working towards decalcifying my pineal gland has stopped my unbearable migraines? I have gone from ten bad ones a year, requiring admission to hospital, to one or two normal migraines a year, if even that. By *normal*, I mean the type that you take a couple of paracetamol tablets and sleep it off, not an emergency admission to hospital by ambulance. How did I reverse or decrease the severity of my allergies? I did it by placing one or two drops of organic pure iodine in a litre of water and drinking it throughout the day. This worked for me, and it was something I stumbled across by chance. I would try different things and if they agreed with me then I would continue. If something did not agree with me then I would try something different.

As I keep travelling on this road to rediscovering me, I am also enjoying reconnecting with real people who feed my soul with their pure hearts, and I have removed shallow and materialistic people from my everyday world. This is the world I belong to. After all, if every one of us on this earth got out of bed every day thinking of something nice we could do for someone else instead of what we can gain or what's in it for us, this would be such a much nicer world to live in.

Along the way, I have also had to deal with people who have ridiculed my way of thinking, telling me I was being reckless because there was no scientific evidence to support my hare-brained health theories. The fact that I have managed to keep myself alive for thirty years with a godawful disease that the medical establishment were only willing to give me twelve months to five years to live is proof enough for me; beyond that, I do not care. In addition, I feel I am getting better and stronger and that I am enjoying my life and my family again. I do not need a scientific study to tell me that I can bounce out of bed on 361 mornings a year as opposed to my previous 50 if I was lucky.

At the end of the day, the scientific prognosis for my condition was not good. I just chose an alternative. It is my right to. For this, I am not going to apologise. It is not as if I am hurting anyone else by choosing an alternative. Considering I am now at eight years post diagnosis and at a much better place than I was in 2010, I know I have done well.

Chapter 8

Visions

I am no Alison Dubois; that is for sure. I wonder how her journey started, but I have had some interesting visions. They are both exciting and frustrating at the same time. I wish they came with a question-and-answer page, making them easier to decipher, but unfortunately, they did not.

Vision 1—Daniel Morcombe

This is the first time I ever was consciously having a vision, and it was about a year after Daniel Morcombe vanished from a bus stop in Queensland. He was abducted from a bus stop close to his home just before Christmas, and he was murdered by a paedophile. One evening, I had been attempting to do some automatic writing where after a meditation I was asking him to help me to find him so we could give his family closure. I asked if he was in spirit, first if he was alive, and I wrote *N* for no.

Then I asked if he was dead, and I wrote a *Y* for yes. I knew I was repeating myself, but I was questioning whether it was genuine or not. Now I had never attempted this before, and I wasn't sure if it was real or if I was just desperate to get something like my higher self and nothing more. After that, I asked where he was, and I wrote "Glass Hause Mountains." This was about a year after his disappearance.

This has always baffled me because, as a Queensland boy, he should have known that was not spelled correctly. My family and I were frequent visitors to the area, so I knew that it was not coming from me. I always wondered if he may have had some confusion with spelling the word *house*. On the other hand, perhaps it was sometimes spelt that way, which is the German spelling of house.

As I was falling asleep that night, I had my first vision. I saw police cars near a dirt track and officers going into bushland and coming out with bags of evidence. I can only describe it like watching a news bulletin, but the sound was turned off. I knew I wasn't asleep because I could actually hear the TV in my bedroom was on and John was watching TV. He was watching a movie, nothing related to what I was seeing.

The police didn't find Daniel Morcombe's remains for nearly ten years after his disappearance. Yes, his remains were at the Glass House Mountains a few kilometres from where he'd gone missing, and, yes, they were in bushland.

This was something I had always wished I could have discussed with his parents, but I didn't want to add to their grief, and as I didn't have any concrete evidence and this was so new to me, I even questioned if it was worth mentioning it. What if I was wrong and wasted police resources? The Glass House Mountains cover a large area. I shared this vision with my family at that time, but no one else.

Vision 2—Amanda Berry

A few years ago, I had seen a distressed post about a man who was missing and his friends were concerned. As it turned out later, the man was found, and no harm had come to him—he had never been "missing." This was both embarrassing and a bit confusing. What made me connect this man to my vision was the fact that he looked like Colonel Sanders and there was a bus in his profile picture.

This was the vision: I saw a young woman with wavy brown hair. She came out of an American-style house. The house was double storey and narrow. It reminded me of houses I had seen in movies in areas around Detroit. If you were facing it from the street, it had a large picture window on the left and a door on the right-hand side and a fly screen on the front of it; it was very narrow, and it was on a street of similar row houses. The woman walked down to the local square and walked into a Salvation Army op shop, all the while looking back to see if I was continuing to follow her. My vision also took me inside the house. It was dirty and dusty, very messy. It looked unloved and horrid. Even though I knew that this woman lived in the house, the interior view looked as if it desperately lacked a woman's touch.

The man who lived in the house reminded me of one of the sleazy characters of *The Texas Chainsaw Massacre*. On the dusty floorboards, I could see a child's toys and a doll. In my head, I was hearing "American house of horrors." I knew this house had a basement and an attic, even though it looked tiny from the outside. Unfortunately I wasn't shown the attic or the basement. I knew that the house had a sinister story to it.

I also saw a school bus, which is why I thought it connected to the missing man's profile. In the lounge room sitting at a small square table, reading a paper was a man who looked like Colonel Sanders.

So here comes the embarrassing part. So what do you do if you think you can help someone in trouble? Do you ring the police Crime Stoppers hotline and sound like another crazy woman thinking she is a psychic?

"Hello, this is Crime Stoppers," says the lovely police officer on the other end of the phone.

"Hi, this is me, and I know this is going to sound crazy, but I think I have some information about a missing man I saw on Facebook."

Oh God, kill me now!

So, I tell the lovely police officer about the "American house of horrors." I described the house as a Detroit-style house. The woman with the wavy brown hair, the kids toys on the floor, my reference to the chainsaw massacre. I describe the house and the Salvation Army op shop and also mentioned the bullying bus and Colonel Sanders, and I'm turning green as I'm speaking, because if I hadn't called anonymously, I would have been expecting people with white coats at my front door.

The officer was very professional, and did not laugh once. Well, not that I could hear anyway. After I had passed on all the information that I could remember, I hung up, feeling stupid and swearing that I would never do something very stupid as to be that nutcase who wastes valuable police resources on stupid whims. I also told him that the house had multiple levels an attic and basement, which isn't really common in Australian homes.

The next day after my call to Crime Stoppers, a young woman with brown wavy hair, two other women, and a child were rescued after ten years in captivity. One of the women had been picked up, while the offender was working as a bus driver on her school run. There was a female child born to the woman who escaped and her captor. In one of his prison photos, he totally looked like the redneck sleazebag from *The Texas Chainsaw Massacre*. Not to mention the house looked exactly like the house in my vision. I would have loved to see internal police pictures of the lounge room, not to mention his DVD collection, to see if *The Texas Chainsaw Massacre* was a favourite of his. Also, the news headline was "American House of Horrors." The Salvation Army op shop was her desperation to be saved from the hell she and the other two women were living in.

A few years later, I actually was wondering where Colonel Sanders came into play here. Perhaps her captor regularly fed them KFC as part of their diet. Who knows?

Interpreting the vision now, her walking into the *Salvation Army* op shop, she was asking someone to save her. No names, no location, and the wrong continent beginning and ending with *A*. What a wild goose chase! I also found out that the house was in Detroit. That was my lack of knowledge of American geography. Oops.

I am sure the lovely police officer would have picked up the form he just filled out and calmly placed it in the file marked "Crackpot."

Vision 3—S'oer Street Signs

I had a vision many years ago. It was of a street sign that had "S'oer Street" written on it. This was a word I'd never heard of before and didn't even know that it existed and still have no idea what I'm meant to do with this, so if you have any ideas please let me know. It apparently has something to do with a street-art movement.

Vision 4—Insulated Child's Room

One day I had another vision, I feel through the eyes of a child. At first I thought the child was in a frozen cool room, but then I realised that it was a room where the walls had been sprayed with expanding foam. Whether this was for insulation purposes or noise-cancelling purposes, I am not sure.

The room looked the size of a shipping container. There was a single bed up against one wall, and at the foot of the bed was a small table with a lamp or vase on it. The room was dimly lit, and I felt frightened, as though I was being kept against my will.

The bed was covered in a girly, floral-print doona cover, and the door looked heavy and had a distinctive red-stencil-type stamp on the wall on the left-hand side of the door. I am not sure if they were Chinese letters, as I was too far away to actually try to read them. It reminded me of the type of stamp you often see on a meat carcass.

I know I have a long way to go on my spiritual journey or awakening, but it's going to be interesting.

I am enjoying the beautiful people coming into my life, and I feel blessed for the experiences that I have had so far and look forward to many more.

Chapter 9

Remote Viewing

This, I have managed to do at least twice that I was aware of. The first time it happened, I was not well, and I was lying on a recliner, just floating between planes, when I found I travelled into some random lounge room. It was obviously a small apartment, and I could hear two young people, probably a couple, in the kitchen. It sounded as if they were putting away groceries and talking. I couldn't make out what they were saying, as it was muffled. I do not know why it happened or what the purpose of the experience was. Why did I see it, and what was I meant to do with it? I never saw their faces, so I will forever be wondering whom these people were and why it happened.

The second time was while my kids were on holiday in America, and they were having an awful time and were very unhappy. I found myself in their hotel room. I could see them and hear them talking, but again, it was muffled. I could see their whole group sitting on the beds and talking before going out sightseeing. I wish I'd taken note of what they were wearing so that I could have had it validated later, but I did remember a young friend who was also there bed hopping, jumping from one bed to the other, which apparently she did do in one of the hotels.

Chapter 10

Reversing Allergies and Sensitivities

As I mentioned before, over the years I found my list of allergies and sensitivities was growing by the day. At this rate, I feared that soon I was going to end up as the "lady in the plastic bubble," sensitive to everything and anything out there in the atmosphere.

As well as all the other difficulties and complications in my life, I often wondered if this was a life worth living.

Fortunately, for me, I am a very strong and resilient person, but even strong people have their limits. We are not superhuman, and at times, you do question if it is worth it. At least I did on many occasions. The fact that you are holding your family back weights you down.

As Mikaela's wedding approached, I also had to deal with the anxiety about whether I would be well enough to attend on the day. Her day would be marred, and she would be so disappointed. I was always feeling guilt about missing any milestones or special occasions. I also resented the fact that all my problems were affecting not only me but also the quality of life of my husband and children. My family, thanks to me, could not plan a basic outing, whether it was a catch-up with friends or a drive to the country. Nothing was ever going to be spontaneous again.

This was like a death anyway for someone like me who was a free spirit. I loved the outdoors and nature, and my garden was my sanctuary and connection to life and earth. In the garden, I was able to escape my pain and get lost in my thoughts. I greatly enjoyed looking at my work after I was done; I found it so rewarding and refreshing.

I happened to notice that shortly after my escapades in the garden, I found myself ill and always with a migraine. This went on for years. I had never made any connection between my migraines and the garden. Shortly after my trip to the allergy specialist, I was diagnosed with a severe sensitivity to an outdoor airborne mould called *cladosporium*. As devastating as this was to me because of my love of the outdoors, it was also a revelation that answered many questions and brought so much to light.

For years, my family and I drove to Queensland for our family holiday. We loved driving through the Australian bush, seeing the animals and the countryside in all its unspoiled beauty. As we drove past freshly ploughed fields, I got the family (from the smog and city life) to put down the car windows and inhale the clean country air. On every single one of those trips, by the time we reached our destination, I was very sick.

Knowing what I know now about my mould allergy, I always turn the car air-conditioning system to recirculating, and it doesn't happen anymore. Or if I want to have the windows open, I can wear a surgical face mask, and it makes such a difference, as do the saline nasal sprays that I use. Forewarned is forearmed. I have implemented a few simple things that make a huge difference to my daily enjoyment of life.

I had sensitivity to lavender, rose, all citrus, jasmine, mint, coriander, and the whole mint family and the cousins too, such as chia seeds, which are part of the mint family. Who knew?

My most severe allergy known to date is to the preservative 220-sulphur dioxide. This is by far my most severe allergy, and an attack from eating something with it always ends with me in hospital. The thought of an attack terrifies me to my core. I am so terrified of the reaction that I avoid it, and thanks to a few slip-ups, I know that this particular sensitivity is still there.

I wish I had a smart phone back in the days before I knew what the trigger was to have kept video of how sick it made me. Every time I had a glass of champagne or a glass of wine, it landed me in hospital. It always amazes me how many different types of foods contain it. Even fruit and meat can be laced with it. Suffice to say, life ended up revolving around reading labels before I could touch anything or eat anything. How I envy people who can just reach into a bowl of lollies and enjoy them without the worry. Sounds simple, doesn't it? However, for me, it is not. It's a minefield.

Solvents and petrochemicals were also problems for me. I noticed fumes from cars, buses, planes, and trucks sent me to bed quite quickly. Even fumes from the lawnmower, whipper snipper, or chainsaw made me sick. This meant Sunday mornings when neighbours were out doing maintenance was an absolute nightmare for me. When my gardener came to clean up our garden, I had to go inside and close all the windows. There are so many things that people take for granted and don't know how lucky they are.

If I woke up in the morning and had a metallic taste in my mouth, I knew that the council had sprayed weedkiller around the nature strips in my area. I did not even have to go outside and see the blue-tinted borders around the footpaths and street signs to know I was right. My eyes would be running and the metallic taste would make me cough and wheeze like an asthmatic.

Someone using a can of fly spray gave me a headache and muscle weakness in my arms and legs. It was instant.

Polyester and perfumes were also sensitivities, totally debilitating ones. I remember nearly grounding an aeroplane because a lady next to me decided to put her peppermint hand lotion on with a particularly strong perfume. I thought I was going to die. I wish people would think before lathering themselves in a lotion. You might love a particular scent, but it does not mean everybody shares your love of the product. Not to mention in a confined space like an aeroplane, there isn't anywhere for someone like me to go.

The same goes for people who enjoy drowning themselves in their favourite perfume or aftershave. Multiply that by every person on an aeroplane and watch me literally gag. I realised while sitting in the allergy specialists' waiting room that I was not alone; I was not unique. There were so many others in the same boat as me. I realised some of the people sitting around me were ten times worse. I wonder what they were doing to cope with daily life.

Again, I nearly grounded a plane after the cabin crew fumigated the aircraft with canisters of some chemical, and I began vomiting uncontrollably out of the blue. I wish I knew what was in that canister, and if the effects were so sudden, I wonder what the long-term damage might be, if any.

Seriously, most people probably find all the above to be trivial, but you have no idea how serious it could be for someone like me with sensitivity.

For many years, because of these allergies, my world was getting smaller and smaller. I avoided shopping centres. I had to try to hold my breath in a florist shop. When I would walk into a shop or a home with a plug-in air freshener or burning incense or oils sent me into nervous-system shutdown. It was everywhere, and it worked against me. At least I could fill my home with fake flowers and keep myself healthy. I could close my windows on windy days and lock myself inside to avoid having a very bad day.

As the allergies multiplied, I was really concerned about where this nightmare was going to end.

About four years ago, I realised my visions stopped coming and were fewer and further between, to virtually non-existent. So using my friend Google, I learned about decalcifying the pineal gland, and I decided to try a few things. At first, I was limited because many of the very things on that list just happened to be things I was sensitive or allergic to: lemon, coriander, and mint. Talk about frustrating. So I got onto all and every other thing that I could do and started doing what I could. The only thing on that list that I didn't think I was allergic to was iodine, so I decided to try it. After all, what did I have to lose?

After six months on the iodine, I was starting to think that it was a waste of time, as I didn't feel any different and there was no obvious change in any way. I was feeling good, but I just put it down to having a good run.

However, quite surprisingly, I noticed that by removing the heavy metals and decalcifying my pineal gland, my sensitivities have reduced and some are closer to non-existent now.

This is why I refer to all the above experiences as a journey, because it really is a road travelled, with hills, cliffs, and all the pitfalls you can imagine—but definitely worth the leap of faith. Had I not decided to do this, I wouldn't be where I am today. I probably wouldn't be here at all.

Yes, it is hard. Yes, at times you feel like you want to crash and burn just to stop the pain and suffering. However, if you did that, you would miss all the beauty and potential that has been sitting there waiting for you the whole time. I would never have met my little granddaughter, and watching her grow is the highlight of my life. I believed becoming a mother was the ant's pants best thing to ever happen to me, but a grandmother was something I had never considered I was going to live long enough to experience. I truly love every single minute of it.

My advice to anyone who thinks that what they've read so far strikes a nerve would be get up every morning with the aches and creaks and keep moving. Every day is a blessing. Do not give up. Research, research, research, and try different things. Use common sense. Try, and keep trying, until you find something that helps you to improve your quality of life. Reversing my allergies was actually a side effect from something else I was trying to do, and it has improved my life by 90 per cent. Isn't that how some of the most miraculous medical discoveries have been achieved, simply by accident?

I can plan and travel again; I can go out for dinners and spend quality time with my family. Life is fun again, and had I been waiting for the medical profession to help me, I know my health would have been getting worse by now, not better.

All I ask is that you use common sense. I had a female friend of my mother's many years ago. This lady had terminal cancer and went to some healer for treatment. She was placed on a lettuce-and-water-only diet. I'm sure in the end she died from starvation rather than the cancer. With four children, she was desperate to get better; she was grasping at straws. Unfortunately she chose the wrong ones. How could a lettuce diet sustain someone who needed to actually be going the other way and feeding her body with nutritious and clean food? It might not have saved her in the end, but I am sure it could have potentially bought her many more years with her family. There is strong evidence on the benefits of fasting to reboot the immune system. However, at some stage you surely will have to provide some nutrients to keep the body functioning.

Chapter 11

Working with the Elderly

Many years ago in my local area, I heard a story that not only moved me to tears but also made me feel ashamed at the state of our society.

An elderly woman living in a suburb of Melbourne about ten minutes from my home at the time was found dead at her kitchen table. Her name was Elsie. Elsie had no children of her own and only one sister with whom she often had fallings-out.

The horrible thing was that by the time Elsie was found she was totally skeletal. Decomposition had occurred, and I thought nobody had missed her, been there for her in her final moments, offered her medical help or support. No one had been there to put her on the floor to make her more comfortable or to hold her hand as she took her last breath or laid her to rest in her final resting place, not spend two years slumped at her kitchen table.

How can this happen in a First World country with all sorts of gadgets, devices, and cameras that can do a thousand things? In suburbia surrounded by houses and people, an elderly woman passed away in her home, and it took two years for her remains to be discovered. To me, this was heart breaking. The fact that there were some elderly people in my community who could go so long without any other human enquiring about them or having any human contact.

Elsie had neighbours who cleaned out her letterbox and shoved her mail under her front door. They would also throw out accumulated brochures, catalogues, and other junk mail. They assumed she had gone off to hospital and then into a care home. After a while, the power and other utilities were disconnected after final warnings and lack of payment. Houses sold; people moved; life outside Elsie's home was going on as usual.

Neighbours continued mowing her lawn and maintaining the outside of her property, keeping it tidy. Nobody knew her well enough to have any further contact numbers of her nearest relative or next of kin.

Her only sister called the house and left messages on her answering machine. When her calls went unanswered, she assumed her sister was being stubborn and still upset with her, and she stopped calling. Eventually the phone was disconnected; Elsie's sister assumed she had changed her phone number.

This story was in my local paper and got me wondering how many other Elsie's were out there. Some elderly people were going days, weeks, or even years without any outside contact. I questioned how I could make a difference, so I started at first becoming a volunteer with my local council. During this time, I saw a massive need for carers. The council had trouble keeping up with the demand, so I decided to become a carer for the elderly and disabled. I was going to help out for a few months; I was there for two years. If my health hadn't decided to deteriorate, I'd probably still be there. It was hands down the most rewarding thing I had ever done in my life. It also gave me the strength to forget my health issues for a little while because others were more desperate than me and they were depending on me.

I made many friends; it didn't feel like a job. I loved our visits, and I really looked forward to them. Some were on a weekly roster, and some fortnightly. I remember some of them saying that youth was wasted on the young, and I totally agreed. I think the visits were the highlight of my day; I would even miss them and sometimes take Ashley over on a weekend for a visit. It was the most rewarding work I had ever, ever done in my life. Some of my clients would have no other human contact, sometimes for weeks at a time.

On a sunny day, I would put my elderly clients in a wheelchair and take them outside for some fresh air and sunshine. Due to their fear of falling, they lose their confidence and fear going outside alone. The weeks, months, and years pass by, and they become more housebound.

At every stage of life, you need to stay positive, roll with the punches, and go with the flow. It is your life, and it is totally your decision how to live it. Do not ever give away your power, who you let in and whom you do not. Own your talents as well as your faults. I need to take on much of my own advice and finally stand up and say what's on my mind.

I can be loud at times, but I always seem to stop myself from saying what I really want to say. By doing that, I might be loud, but I'm not being true to myself or ever really being heard. Do not decide to change your ways tomorrow. Start now. Start right now. Do not waste one precious minute.

What I have come to understand is how little people close to me really know about me and what is important to me, but at the end of the day, that is not their fault. If I did not acknowledge myself, how will they ever know the real me if I choose to not speak up for myself?

Another valuable saying I heard once long ago is that life is not a rehearsal. You don't get to do it again. Working with the elderly, hearing them reminisce about their youth, made me realise that life passes in what seems to be a blink of the eye. Now looking back on my own life so far, I realise how true that is.

My greatest memory with an elderly male client called Albert went like this: On a wet and stormy day, I went to his house in heavy, pelting rain. Albert greeted me with a beaming smile and the most booming "Good morning" that I had ever heard.

I replied, "Is it?"

"But of course," he roared back. "I woke up this morning, and I wasn't in a box; that makes it a very good morning. I could see the sky."

How right he was. His zest for life taught me to appreciate every minute, good or bad, and to realise that there is always a positive aspect. It's just a matter of what you choose to focus on. Now when I see someone struggling while going through a hard time, I tell them this story.

Many will remember Albert, and hopefully they will then share this story with others. Every time I see my elderly neighbour Walter, who is ninety-four years old, I say good morning and ask him how he is. His response is always "I can see the sky, Celeste. I can see the sky."

Whether Albert is still alive or not, his philosophy is still putting a smile on the faces of others and reminding them that things aren't that bad.

Every time I thought I was having a really bad day, I'd gently remind myself that I could see the sky, so I knew that I was going to get through this, and this was going to pass. It helped me put things in perspective to realise that every day I had a choice—good day or bad day. It was up to me.

Chapter 12

Gratitude

Every day I thank the universe for all that I have—my life, my family, my friends, food on the table, the clothes on my back, and slowly but surely getting my health back. Everything else is a bonus.

I thank God for the air in my lungs and for giving me the strength to get to this point. If I can look out at the sky, then that is great. I'm already winning.

I have seen one grandchild, and I was there to help my mum though major heart surgery in the beginning of 2015. I was also there and able to care for her and hold her hand when she took her last breathes in February 2019. I am blessed and grateful every day, but not for material things—they are not important to me and never were. Life can be great, and life can be not so great. As the saying goes, if life gives you lemons, make lemonade.

I remember on my darkest days that I did not care about any of the material things in my life. I couldn't care less about anything but getting through, surviving the day. I thought how sad that we need to get that sick to realise the importance of the simple things. The best things in life really are free. Unfortunately, we waste a lifetime chasing material goals, and it takes a reality check—or, in my case, illness—to slap me back into the real world.

If times have been tough, focus on the positives and don't let the negatives get you down. They can drown you if you let them. Attitude is everything. Your attitude determines how you deal with something and how you heal or how fast you heal. It is up to you. The more laughter you have in your life, the easier the tough days will be to overcome.

I also understood what some cancer patients mean when they say that cancer was the best thing that ever happened to them. Some people only really start living after the doctor tells them that they might die. In my case, it was a bit different—all I wanted was a name for my condition, because up until then, no one took me seriously, and I was beginning to believe that maybe it was all in my head. Pardon the pun.

Once I had a name for my illness, I knew exactly what I was facing, and that made it easier. All I had to do was boost my immune system, and that is exactly what I did. At the end of the day, I didn't need anyone's approval or permission, and I didn't need to feel guilty about my decision. It was my life, and I didn't need to answer to anyone but me.

I could easily have thrown my hands up in the air and given up, but I had so many people relying on me and supporting me that it motivated me to keep fighting and keep trying to improve my health. I also believe you attract more of what you fear, so if you wake up in the morning thinking you are not going to have a good day, then you probably will not, because of all the negativity you will have attracted to yourself. So regardless of how miserable I felt, I tried to think of all the things I was going to do on a better day and focus on positive things. My bathroom mirror became a whiteboard for daily affirmations, which also had a flow-on effect for my family.

One day, Ashley asked me to move the affirmations as they were in her way when she applied her make-up and the resounding *no* came from the two most unlikely male members of the household my husband and Ashley's partner. Their reactions surprised me.

Remember: it does not matter how bad you think your life is; there is always someone out there doing it tougher. So always, go back to gratitude for the good things and positive things in your life.

I'll never forget the day that all our material possessions—our valuable antique furniture, paintings, photos, luggage, everything that we didn't have room to take with us—went into storage and I locked the door and walked out of the storage facility. I had a light-bulb moment when I realised it was just stuff. If anything, I felt it was weighing me down, but I was struggling to let it go. So what did we do? We paid $1,500 for the removalist to get it into storage. Over the next six years, we paid $17,000 for the facility. Then $1,000 for the removalist to deliver what was left of it to my parent's home six years later when I was feeling better so that I could sort through it, and then I ended up selling half of it and giving the rest away because I just wanted it gone.

If I was to be totally honest with you, the thought of that stuff actually nauseated me every time I looked at it. It was excessive and irrelevant, and I realised none of that was important. So now my girls know I put no value on material possessions. When I do go, I don't want them hanging on to my furniture and creating a shrine in their homes holding on to my stuff like many people do, becoming hoarders, holding on the grandma's china cabinet, mum's bed, Auntie Judy's cat portraits, and leaving no room for anything of theirs. You can always take a picture and keep it in a keepsake box. You do not need to hang on the half the house.

So be grateful for everything good and bad as it shapes who you are. Stuff is not important; it is just baggage. It is not you or what defines you, and it does not make you complete. For me, I came to realise it was a burden, and my family was all I really needed to complete me. As long as my family and I were under the same roof, that was all that was important nothing else.

Hard as my journey has been, I'll never regret any of it, and at the end of the day, I'm proud of the person who has walked out at the other end, and I'm grateful for all that I've learned along the way. I may not have climbed Everest, but I've climbed an Everest of my own, and now as I'm typing this, I'm visualising myself rolling down that mountain through grass and flowers, laughing like a three-year-old. Who cares how stupid I might look? Yes, I'm going to come down that mountain any which way I want. Why? Because I can! I have been to hell and back; I am not going to waste another valuable precious minute overthinking things.

I also remembered when we were newlyweds, saying to John I really did not care if I lived in a caravan so long as I had my health and my family around me. This I actually felt from the bottom of my heart. So whatever happened to that girl? Where did she lose her way?

Chapter 13

Forgiveness

Unfortunately I'm not that evolved this may be a chapter that I might have to revisit at a later stage.

Have I forgiven those who have wronged me throughout my life? I am not sure, but what I have decided to move on and not waste another second of my life on them. They are no longer renting space in my head. They were not worth the time of day then, and they certainly are not now.

I have also acknowledged that karma takes care of things, and I have noticed things are being taken care of in their natural order. I have a better understanding of divine timing, and I understand why things happened to me this way. Had they happened earlier, I would not have been ready to fight, and I would have just accepted what doctors told me, and because of organ failure, I would not be here now.

I believe there is a higher being that will take care of matters, so it is not for me to wish anything bad on anyone or wish them harm. By their own actions, they start that ball rolling themselves. I've known people to rob innocent people out of inheritances only to lose it all in bad business decisions. That's just karma doing its job.

Have you heard a saying about "when karma comes around, I hope I get a front-row seat"? I do not really want a front-row seat because it does not give me joy to watch someone suffer. However, it is what they put out, so it is what they are going to get back. It has nothing to do with me.

About ten or so years ago, I had a situation unfold, and I just knew it was going to happen, which might explain why I was so calm in my dealing with it; it was a very difficult time for our family.

John, Ashley, and I were on holiday in Malaysia, when I received a call from Mikaela who had stayed behind because of university commitments.

She was distraught, and she was in tears. She had had a disagreement with a family friend, Joe, and she was ordered to get out of the car and abandoned, a ten-minute drive from home and a ten-minute walk from their destination.

She was hysterical because she was alone and didn't know what to do and he had been really mean to her. I spoke to her and tried to calm her down. I was eight or nine hours away by aeroplane—what else could I do? I told her he had issues and not to worry as it was his problem not hers. He was a person with serious anger management issues.

As I eventually hung up the phone, John looked at me and said, "I bet you want to kill him right now."

I looked at him calmly and said quite simply, "No, I don't want to kill him." Now do not get me wrong, I would do anything for my kids, but I just said to my husband not to worry about me. I was going to get my justice, but I clearly told him then and there that it was going to come from a higher source, not from me. They were my exact words.

I felt as though I was having an out-of-body experience. Why was I so calm? What was happening to me? Normally I would have had much to say under these circumstances, at the very least a ten-minute rant.

I just knew (that obviously was the knowing thing at play here) that he would be getting exactly what he deserved, and I wasn't going to have to lift a finger. My calmness was so surprising even to me.

Twenty minutes later, I received another call from Mikaela, but this time, she was laughing. I listened in disbelief as she explained to me what had happened after her first call. After being reprimanded by his family members in the car, Joe turned around and picked her up again and drove her to the original destination.

They went to the hospital to visit a family member who had had major heart surgery. Upon entering the room, Joe fainted. As Mikaela got out of the elevator, all she could see was two massive feet and a mountain of man who apparently came down like a tonne of bricks, sending hospital staff running around like maniacs, and calling code blue all over the PA system. He was so embarrassed and sore after this incident; it took him weeks to recover. Karma isn't a bitch; she is fair, so if you do the wrong thing, expect a visit.

I understand it was a very traumatic time for everyone, but that does not make it OK to terrorise a teenager just because you are stressed. They were all under stress; that was no excuse. That's just being a bully.

Karma came to the party, but I must admit not even I had expected such a quick result.

When we make our bed, we then have to lie in it. What we put out; we get back at the end of the day. It really is simple.

My focus has always been my family, and if I can offer some help to someone in need, in the way of an ear or a shoulder to lean on for support, I will. I don't judge. I understand the complexities of life and relationships. I also know how quickly we can find ourselves in a foreign position dealing with things we would never have imagined.

Gossip is such a negative energy and a waste of time. If you see someone struggling, offer friendship, not judgement. If you have time to gossip, then you have an unfulfilled and very sad life. You just never know when life is going to serve you a curveball and you will need that ear or shoulder yourself.

Chapter 14

Priorities

I had never much given any thought to the word *priority* until I got sick. Up until then, keeping house, keeping kids clean, busy to and from school activities, shopping, cooking, cleaning, running my property development business, keeping up with my business paperwork and school newsletters, as well as all the household paperwork accounts, and so on kept my head spinning. Just keeping up with the everyday, mundane stuff was a massive challenge.

My only priority at the time was not to drown in my daily planner.

After life hit the proverbial fan, my biggest priority was whether someone was going to be home by three in the afternoon so that I could have a shower or if I had money in my wallet so that I could send one of the kids out to bring home some dinner for everyone or to order in. This was before Menulog or Uber Eats. We have come so far, as back then our only delivery option was pizza.

I will never forget thinking how different the meaning of the word *priority* was between one person and another. I am not judging, because before this experience, I probably was the same.

I remember having had an awful afternoon. My doctor had just finished telling me in front of Ashley, who was fourteen at the time, that, yes, I had been diagnosed with a "godawful disease" and that my prognosis was twelve months as a worst-case scenario if my organs did not cope with the medication I was going to be placed on. The best-case scenario was five years until my organs began shutting down due to the toxicity of the medication and it was the kidneys that usually failed first.

I wasn't shocked by the diagnosis because I'd been telling anyone who would listen that I wasn't feeling well, so this came as no shock to me. If anything, it was a relief that I was not an idiot or a hypochondriac—my symptoms were real. Unfortunately, the thing about many autoimmune diseases is that they are internal, so it is not as if you walk around with crutches or bandages that people can see. So often, you have nothing to show for the misery that you feel daily. After the doctor's diagnosis, my poor little girl went into shock. After all, I was her mum, strong and invincible. This could not be happening. I was her superhero. How could I be so sick?

At this particular time, a million things were running through my head, finances, whether my husband was going to be able to make ends meet without my contribution. What was going to happen to them ten years from now? How they were going to cope, how my kids were going to cope with my funeral and my death when it came. We had always been a two-income family, and we were used to a great life.

I was scared that this would affect my kids, their educations, and the lives they had become accustomed. That afternoon, a thousand new worries had jumped to the front of the line and taken on lives of their own. I remember feeling as if the whole sky had just dropped on my head.

Then a friend dropped in. She knew I was ill and that I had just had an important doctor's appointment, so she came to see how I was, or so I thought. However, she actually came to show me her new Maserati. She then wondered why I wasn't updating my car. I think that at that point my car was about ten years old. It was not a problem for me, but it obviously a concern for her. I remember looking at her and watching her lips move, but it was like I'd gone deaf. Was she for real? Didn't she listen to anything I had just said?

At this point I realised exactly what was wrong with my life or more so the people I'd embraced and referred to as friends.

I had explained to her the severity of my situation and the diagnosis and all she could say was "Oh well, when you get better."

Please explain to me what a bed-ridden person who had not driven in three months needed with a new car, especially if my doctor's prediction was correct and I only had twelve months to live. Was she serious? This was someone I had considered one of my closest friends.

I realised then that she was not only, not listening, but she did not care. Furthermore, I don't think she heard a word of what I'd just told her or understood what I was going through or the enormity of what I was facing.

I also remember planting things in my garden and thinking, *Are my children going to enjoy this and appreciate it when it flowers, or is it going to go unnoticed? Where will I be by the time this or that comes in to flower?* My husband has no interest in the garden other than wanting it to look good. He had never noticed until after we moved out that we had an arbour with a mature purple wisteria growing over it that I had planted more than seven years previously. Any gardener knows wisterias take forever to settle and flower. He hadn't even noticed it. This is why I never wondered if he was going to enjoy anything I was planting, as it was something he had no interest in. He liked the garden to look good and manicured to within an inch of its life, but that was about it.

Nothing was stable, and the ground was constantly shifting under my feet.

Life had certainly changed for us. At this time, I also started looking at the people in my life through different eyes. It was as though I was seeing them for the first time. I remembered the parties where people walked up to me and ask me how I was, and before I could answer, they were looking past my ear at who else was around. So I realised they were not genuine, and I stopped telling people how I was. For the first time in my life, I started declining invitations that I had previously accepted because I felt obligated to.

Chapter 15

Death/Fear of Dying

I am often asked whether I fear dying, and the answer is no. I'm happy with all I've achieved in my life, and with all my NDEs and all the times in the past that I thought this might be it, I know that when my time is up, it's up. Whether I die in my sleep from a blood clot or get hit by a bus, there will be nothing I can do about it. It will be my time, my divine timing once again.

I understood why it took the medical establishment thirty years to finally diagnose my symptoms and give me a name for it. The reason was there was no Google. Now had I been diagnosed thirty years ago, I would have taken the medication that was prescribed because I would have been none the wiser. Therefore, I would not be here now. I would have been at the mercy of my doctors and done exactly what I was told. Again, by preventing the diagnosis, my guides were again protecting me.

Just as easily as going to see the doctor for one thing and by chance being diagnosed with something else, which in a nick of time saves your life, I also believe the forces from beyond can hinder a diagnosis if the timing is not right. This is what I believe happened to me. That annoying divine timing that plays its part in your life, in the background, with you none the wiser. A friend of mine took her three-year-old to the doctor for a summer cold, and as her doctor was walking them out of his office, he noticed a melanoma on her exposed shoulder and instantly sent her off for a biopsy. It was extremely lucky that it was caught early, and since this was brought to her attention, they found others that also needed ongoing monitoring or surgery. Had she taken her child in winter, she may never have known until it was too late. Melanoma is such a fast-growing tumour, it needs action and quickly.

So in my case, when that bus with the destination "pearly gates" pulls up to the kerb, and there's a ticket waiting for me, I'll know that my work here is done and that it's OK for me to get on board.

I am also well aware of the fact that even though that god-awful disease is in remission, the blood clots that my body still continues to throw can still at any time cost me my life. Therefore, my family and I have discussed my wishes if something were to happen. I have suffered multiple DVTs and multiple clots in the superficial veins. Out of all those DVTs, only one of the DVTs corresponded with an aeroplane trip, but my specialist was not convinced it was because of the flight.

I refuse to stop travelling, and my reason for this is that life is too short, and if I am meant to die on a plane, I will. I can just as easily die in my bed at home in my sleep. Therefore, I have made it clear to my family that they understand my wishes, and were something to happen on one of our trips, my husband is to arrange for my cremation and bring me back in a cute little box and scatter me under a beautiful jacaranda tree. I refuse to be plonked on a mantle just to choke on dust, or palmed off from one family member to the next. Most of all, I don't like clutter. I am a less-is-more kind of woman.

Not only that, but also my kids will know that I'm happy with all that I've achieved and that I've somehow made a difference to the lives of others and know that there's no doubt that I'm OK with this, and this is what I want. They will never have to second-guess what I might have wanted or if their father had made the right choices at the time.

Chapter 16

An Empath's Work Is Never Done

Being the bright spark that I am (sarcasm), I took a long time to make the connection between high and low vibrations. I heard this phrase all the time, but I could not grasp what it meant.

Nor that walking into certain venues or buildings would or could affect me on an energy level to such an extent. For example, a hospital is draining, as I can feel lots of pain and suffering. I'd always be exhausted and achy after a hospital visit, and often, I would rather stay home than go out and expose myself to negativity. At the end of the day, I had so much already going on around me, suffocating me that I did not need to attract more.

This is how I have come to understand it:

High vibration/happy/positive

Low vibration/sad/negative

I've recently made the connection that places like hospitals, courts, doctors, and many other buildings leave me drained and anxious.

I also have learned to cleanse my home more frequently from negative energies, and when my kids come home, they know I've done a cleansing or clearing, as they can feel the difference in the energy levels in the house immediately. The mood is instantly lighter, and it is good for all in the home, to not only protect the residents from their own energy but also from the heavy or negative energies bought in by others.

When your friends visit and bring in their problems, they leave some of that negativity behind. Over time, this accumulates and leaves behind a heavy blanket or fog.

Empaths feel this; that is why cleansing is so important.

As an empath, I have also come to realise how many energy vampires I had in my life, people who emotionally drained me on a daily basis with their constant negativity doom-and-gloom attitudes. This had to change, and by getting sick, many of these energy vampires went on to find new hosts to live off because they were not getting any more energy from me.

The other thing I continue to find frustrating is that when someone close to me is hurting. I know they're hurting, but at the same time, I know they're extremely private and don't like sharing their private business, and although they are great at being there for me in my time of need, I can't do the same for them. I'm learning to respect their right to privacy and not dwell on it as much as I used to. We are all different. All I could do was keep telling them that I am there if they need me and leave the ball in their court.

On one of our trips to Greece in 2015, I found myself in the midst of a humanitarian crisis of an unimaginable scale. We disembarked from a ferry on the Island of Lesvos and literally walked into a tent city.

The Syrian refugee crisis was no longer something I saw on the news; it was all around me. The fear, the pain, it was gut wrenching, and it was all around me. I was overwhelmed. John went to arrange a hire car while I sat with our luggage. I started crying uncontrollably and could not stop. I felt the desperation of every single man, woman, and child on that port. It was the most overwhelming tragedy I found myself in the middle of.

Mikaela was pregnant at that stage, and I saw young girls her age heavily pregnant or with infants napping on pieces of cardboard on the hot tar in the carpark of the port. It was about thirty-six degrees that day, and even at ten thirty in the morning, it was already hot. A baby approximately three months old was sleeping on cardboard. I had the sense of an aerial picture from above looking down over the tent city of pain and despair. I came home and every time I watch something on TV about the refugee crisis, I'm once again back there walking in a sea of refugees, crying and feeling every one of the emotions I felt that day, and again I feel as if I'm soaring through the sky looking down on this tent city of despair again and again.

Chapter 17

Grief and Regrets

Just as I thought this book was done and dusted, the thunderbolt called life decided to rock my world, and not in a good way, once again.

I'd had a difficult life after what could only have been described as a blessed childhood, with many challenges thrown my way, and by hook or by crook, I overcame them one by one. Illness just being one of them, I thought they were huge, and overall I had to dig deep to find the strength to battle each and every obstacle. Somehow I would drag myself up and keep going. Kids are a great motivator in one's life, as it is no longer about you. It no longer matters if you don't have the energy to get out of bed. You have to get out of bed—kids need to go to school or activities, shopping needs to be done, bills need to be paid, and stuff just has to happen.

Although things had been tough and seemed insurmountable at times, nothing could ever be as bad as the past two weeks.

This is the story of an angel of a boy who came into my life; the son of two wonderful friends. This beautiful blonde boy with the biggest blue eyes you could ever imagine was born in early 1999. He was a beautiful baby, and I remember that every time I picked him up as a new born he fell asleep in my arms. It became a private joke between his mother and me that I always bored him to tears. His name was Ryan.

Our families were close, our children were good school friends, and as often happens when you have children at school, you develop your own little networks of support. For play dates and excursions, school pickups, and helping out when nannies and so on were not available, we were always there for each other.

Eventually, for one reason or another, this beautiful family moved away and distance saw us drift apart and lose touch. I was buried in my own hell and isolation because of illness, and they moved to rural Victoria on a new adventure and a new life.

Over the years, the kids have been fortunate enough to remain connected on Facebook, which was wonderful, and they had been keeping in touch. On one such thread when the kids were chatting, I couldn't help myself. I had to say hi to Ryan. I so loved his energy. He emanated a bright light, and he was so open and friendly. I do not think I had seen him since he had been in early primary school. I was sure he wouldn't remember me. I had such an urge to send him a friend request, but I didn't.

A little while after that chat, I ran into Ryan and his dad in a store in our old neighbourhood. It was by sheer luck we ran into each other, as we hadn't seen each other for at least ten years, and neither of us still lived in the area. I was blown away again by his warmth and his glow. He was bright, compassionate, and so beautifully mannered. It was all I could do not to squash him with a long lost auntie hug. He was so tall, not a little boy anymore. I wanted to, but I didn't.

A short time after this I received a call from Ashley in tears, telling me Ryan, her little school buddy, was gone. Our world fell apart. Today, we still cannot understand why such a beautiful soul loved by so many could be feeling as low as to take his own life.

These are my regrets. On two occasions, I felt compelled to add him as a Facebook friend and talk to him. The nagging little voice in my head was screaming at me to add him, but I was worried that he might think it weird, so I didn't.

Then I remembered the day I ran into him with his dad. I felt like a strong connection when he saw me. Ryan had superpowers; he made everyone he met feel as though they were special. When he was speaking to you, you had his complete and undivided attention. This is so rare in someone of this age, especially a boy. Usually all you get from a teenager, if you were lucky, is a grunt.

Not Ryan. He made you feel as though you were special and that talking to you was the highlight of his life.

On the day of his funeral service, I found out that although he was young, he did in fact have superpowers. From the age of three, he had told his parents that he could see people's colours. Little Ryan was able to see people's auras. Did he see this connection in me in my aura? Was that the connection I was feeling, or was he just being Ryan there for everyone?

All through the school years when someone was sad and sitting alone on a bench, little Ryan was right there beside them making them laugh and giving out a hug or two. He was always getting into trouble because he was giving so many hugs; the teacher thought it was becoming a problem.

I will forever regret not sending that friend request and I will always be left wondering if we had spoken on this topic of spiritual development, I would have been able to introduce him to people who would have been able to teach him protection from overwhelming burdens. Empaths have to learn to switch off from these from time to time. As well as dealing with modern-day stresses faced by kids growing up in our society.

Ryan, I believe, was experiencing some bullying at school, so again, if we were able to chat, I might have picked up on this and offered some solutions for him. I will never know if I may have been able to make a difference, and I am left wondering.

I've lost people who I've grieved for in my extended family, but nothing compares to the loss of a sixteen-year-old a month shy of his seventeenth birthday with a heart of gold and the most infectious smile, who left behind a thousand broken hearts and overwhelming grief. I just hope he could see what I saw at his funeral, an entire cinema filled with family and friends more than seven hundred people there to celebrate his amazing spirit and to pray for his journey, and most of all, that he finally finds peace.

I will forever regret not listening to the nagging inner voice in my head, pushing me to say hello. The planet earth just lost some of its shine.

Five months after his funeral service, I was playing around on my phone and found myself scrolling through my phone when I spotted a message I'd never noticed before. It was dated August 11, 2015; it was from Ryan. It must have been shortly after that post talking with all the kids. This gorgeous human had sent me a friend request and his mother's phone number so we could reconnect. He was forever the bigger person, with that big heart of gold to match. As I type, I finally am able to allow the tears to flow; five and half months after his passing, I accepted his friend request.

Even from the other side, he is able to answer my question that he didn't think it weird at all. I'd obviously wasted time overthinking things.

No do-over-no replay-no rehearsal-just a missed opportunity, and a lifetime of regret.

Chapter 18

Is This the End?

As I approach the end of my journey thus far, yes, I have put things on paper that I have never shared with anyone before.

I have finally decided to start living life again for me. My parents didn't give me life, and my spirit guides didn't go out of their way to keep me alive for me to be anyone's doormat. I have a voice, and I am here to be happy and make a difference in the world. I do matter as a person, and I have my own identity.

I might not be here for a long time, but you can bet your ass I am going to have a good time. I am going to enjoy my family. I'm definitely going to stop sweating the small stuff; after all, after facing death so many times, what I do know is that every minute is precious. Do not just make it your mantra; make it the ultimate to-do list.

For the first time in my life, I have actually started ticking off things on my bucket list, things for me and only me.

I went to a Kiss concert. I don't think I've spent money on a music concert since I was a teenager. I also purchased music on my credit card from iTunes, simply for my entertainment. This is no big deal for most people, but this is how deep not doing things for me ran. For me, it was a massive deal, as if I was taking from my family. A block I put up all on my own, like many others I have discovered along this journey.

All of the above might sound trivial, but to me, it was significant. Most people just add songs to their playlist without giving it a second thought.

I am so happy that I decided to write this story, and, yes, I have learned a lot about myself good and bad.

I am not perfect that I know, but I will live out my days trying to do right by me as well as everyone around me. So please don't tell me I'm opinionated just because I finally speak up and say something that you don't agree with. Ultimately, do not forget it is OK to agree to disagree. I respect your opinion. I only ask that you also respect mine. The reason I say this is that I was surrounded by people who were happy to give you their opinion on something but became argumentative if you tried to share yours. To the point that it was easier to just listen and shut up, as it wasn't worth saying anything or listening to rants. If you can't be yourself, this is where you start losing your voice or right to speak and share your beliefs.

If dealing with chronic illness is not bad enough, the last thing someone like me needs is to deal with negative people who think it is their place to tell you what you should be doing. I am sick of people constantly telling me that God only gives you as much as you can handle. I personally would like to ask him to lighten up. Enough is enough. It is even more difficult to deal with such comments, especially when the advice comes from people who have not suffered as much as a headache in their lives.

We are human, we are challenged every day, and some people seem to be dealt a heavier hand than others are. We are not perfect; we are vulnerable, and often we feel exposed emotionally. We forget all the horrible ways our world has changed. We live in a society where we are more isolated in some ways and then vulnerable and exposed in others.

Social media like Facebook and Twitter, while lifelines for me during my hard times and isolation, can be sources of heartache and bullying platforms for trolls and others.

Gone are the days of the village where everyone is there looking out for one another—the brother, the sister, the cousin, the neighbour the entire community, all looking out for the needs of those around them. Those days are really long gone. There is the saying that it takes a village to raise a child, and I believe it is so true.

If there was a child with a disability, there was always support for the family. If you knew a neighbour had been unwell, the villagers would then take it in turn to provide a cooked meal for the family. Special needs people always had someone looking out for them and were part of the community. They were not isolated or institutionalised as tends to happen now and plastered with labels and shoved into pigeonholes.

I saw this first hand on my regular trips to Greece. In the quiet little village where my mother was born, there is a young man most probably in his mid-forties by now. We noticed him the first time we went with the family in 2002 and every time after that. We watched him interact with the other villagers. Everybody knew him by name; everybody stopped to talk to him and greeted him with love and warmth. He was constantly given bags of fresh produce to drop off to one person or another.

It struck me straight off that this young man would never know loneliness or boredom or isolation like our young people in the same situation would. He would go home at night and feel useful, like he had a purpose. The villagers kept him busy, and judging by the beautiful smile on his face, he was happy too. In our First World lives, the keyboard warriors would be up in arms, saying he is being exploited or devalued or another hundred negative reasons why this should not be happening. Here we go again with the overthinking everything.

We now live in a society where we might not even know the family who lives next door to us, even though we have lived beside them for years.

If this sounds familiar to you, remember all of this can be changed, not tomorrow but today. Does that sound simplistic? Maybe it is, or is it that nowadays we overthink things by design? Is it politically incorrect or correct? Is it offensive? Is it this, or is it that? Seriously, by the time we think about whether to talk to our neighbours, they will have probably moved on.

I am just throwing in a bit of food for thought. Who knows? It just might motivate someone out there to change a few things in their life that they might not be happy with, causing them to introduce themselves to the neighbour, they haven't talked to for many years. Turning a blind eye is easy, but then you wake up old, and your life is coming to an end, and all you can think of are all the things that you wish you had done and all the regrets that are weighing on your soul.

Why do this? Do not wait until you are about to take your last breath to make changes in your life; do it now. I know it all sounds gloomy, but you do not always know when your end is coming, so it is not as if you can say, "Oh, wait, there's something I have to do first."

My time working with the elderly was precious because time and time again every single one of them said that life passed in the blink of an eye, and now, after my experience, looking back at what I've gone through, I totally understand what they mean.

Life is not a rehearsal, so there is no do-over. Get it right the first time. If you are not happy about something, change it. I have also realised the amount of people living loveless marriages and wonder why. That really should be another book. Alternatively, they perhaps need to go over the life-is-too-short chapter. I can't believe I lived and associated with such shallow people in my world. No wonder it was eating me up on the inside, slowly but surely. These people were not my tribe. But yet they walked in and out of my home, my sanctuary, every day, polluting it with their negative energy.

Isn't it unfortunate that it had to take chronic illness to open my eyes and ears and to reconnect not only physically but also spiritually and to show me that I had the right to choose whom to have or not have in my daily life if I did not want to?

Illness is not going to overtake me; nor am I going to dwell on it. I came, I saw, I conquered, and now I am looking forward to a new beginning and the next stage of my life. If I can motivate one person to take life by the horns and not give up, then that is great. That alone makes it all worth it.

Learn to take deep breaths. While I was in the pits of despair, I realised I was holding my breath without even realising it. The body needs oxygen to keep it alkaline. Do not forget to breathe and stop to smell the roses, and often. On the other hand, in my case, maybe not overly deep breaths, because of the allergy thing, but you know what I mean. If you happen to be driving past the beach, stop and watch the waves. Daydreaming is meditation, five minutes, ten minutes, while breathing in some of the sea air. If you made an effort to do that once a week, surely it would help improve your health or at least your sleep.

It's not the end of the world, and life is too short for regrets. Every day has the potential to be a new beginning, and it just depends on you and what you choose to focus on. Don't forget to be kind to the people you come into contact with every day. We all have a story, and you never know what someone else is dealing with.

Cherish life and marvel at the everyday beauty in everything around you and show gratitude always. The most important thing that I have learned is do not forget to tell your family and friends how much you love them every day. You just never know when they just might not come home to you or you to them.

I am also going to stop trying to convince people that I know what I am doing in terms of getting myself healthy. The fact that I am here and healthy yet again should be all the scientific proof I need to offer. At the end of the day, the road I chose to take worked for me, and I shouldn't have to apologise for it or be ridiculed in snide posts on social media. If you have something to say, say it to me directly. Do not hide behind snide cloak-and-dagger comments. Just pray that you are blessed to never walk in my shoes or find yourself distrusting conventional medicine. At the end of the day, I don't owe anyone an explanation. It's not just me you may know others walking the same path. Some people mean well but in reality have no idea what they are talking about.

As I have said right through this book, our personal experiences are what shape us, and each one of us walks a different path. Therefore, it is not really for anyone to judge. People close to me had no idea what I was going through because they never bothered to really try and understand what was wrong with me.

During my journey, I have seen the good, the bad, and the ugly side of humanity.

In 2010, I was finally diagnosed and given a name for what was slowly killing me from the inside. In 2011, my family and I had reached the end of the road and moved out of our home for backup support. At this time, I had to deal with people making up stories because they didn't know what was going on.

It was ugly, it was gossip, and it was hurtful. It was cases of not letting the truth get in the way of a good story. I have not looked back. I have no regrets, and I am no longer going to carry petty, backward people around as baggage. At the end of the day, what I was really going through was ten times worse than anything they were dreaming up. We choose our friends much better these days and are loving life again. If I were to have a small regret, it would be that I did not pay attention after the first lady approached me and having wasted so much time. Nevertheless, there you go: such is life!

Thank you for sharing my journey and picking my book, but then again maybe my book picked you. Everything happens for a reason, and when we need information or guidance, all we need to do is ask, and we shall receive it.

It has amazed me every time on this journey in the way information just comes to me exactly when I need it.

I need to listen to my guides and ask for guidance more often and so should you.

The End

(Or so I thought!)

Chapter 19

The Truth, the Whole Truth, and Nothing but the Truth

OK, so I obviously was not listening again. Again, we booked a trip to Bali, and again we had to cancel and rebook our tickets for the third time because of work commitments. My manuscript was ready to go, and I even emailed my publisher to say that when I got back from Bali I was ready to start the process. While the words "The End" were rolling off the printer, it happened again.

It was about two in the morning on August 2, 2016, and I was excited because finally, later that morning, we were to fly to Bali for a long-awaited break. When I checked my messages, there was one from Mikaela drawing my attention to volcanic ash cloud affecting flights out of Melbourne travelling to Bali.

Some flights the previous day had either been returned to Melbourne or diverted to Darwin. *Surely, this is not happening again*, I thought. Travellers to Bali were being encouraged to contact the airline before making their way to the airport. The airline was not making any promises. Our flight wasn't scheduled to take off till nine that morning, if at all.

While killing time at the airport, I walked into a bookstore as I always do when travelling to stock up on reading material. Besides, that is my idea of a perfect holiday—an endless book supply, a banana lounge pool, and a pineapple juice with an umbrella in it in my hand.

I chose two new releases, just in case the other three books from home were not enough to see me through our ten-day holiday.

After all that stress and angst, our flight ended up leaving on time, no drama at all.

On the flight, I began reading a book written by a young woman named Jaycee Dugard, *A Stolen Life*. At the age of eleven, she had been kidnapped on her way to school and kept prisoner by her abductor. Firstly, I was disturbed at the horror inflicted on an eleven year-old child. As I kept reading, things became apparent to me—how similar the vein in which her book and mine had been written. Although our experiences may have been very different, the story, the paralysed will, conditioning, loss of identity, and loss of voice were the same. What also was paramount in both our stories was our drive to protect our children from the very dangers we were facing on a daily basis. Her book was talking to me, her honesty, her fears, and her loss of voice.

While she was a child taken at the age of eleven, I was annoyed with myself because I was an adult. I couldn't understand why I had no power to change my situation. It was almost as though I was glued to the spot with my feet nailed to the floor. I felt that leaving and removing me from my situation was an insurmountable decision. I had taken vows that I did not take lightly. I felt leaving and taking my children was not an option. Was I trapped because of cultural upbringing or conditioning? Here I was, vowing to write a book about my life, health, spirituality, and struggles, and yet I was going to omit a massive chunk of my life so as to not ruffle feathers or make others uncomfortable.

What about me? Don't I own my own life and experiences?

The more I thought about it, the more I felt like a fraud. I started this book promising myself and you a journey of honesty and self-discovery. Reading this story, I realised that my journey was never going to improve until I found my voice *totally* and completely and was able to voice all the things that over the years I had been made to cover up. Don't get me wrong: no one stuck tape over my mouth or locked me in a room. My life was nothing like hers, but figuratively I was trapped in my own kind of hell and prison.

I didn't want to disappoint my parents or my kids.

This young woman made the same references I did. In several places, she said that with life you do not get to do a do-over. She also spoke of mantras. I felt that even though they were cliché phrases and the very words that I also used, I related to her words and wondered how many others would relate. After the unspeakable things this poor woman faced and survived, I thought I was a gutless wonder and a fraud.

At this point, I realised that by not including the thirty years of trauma that I had faced, I was again not honouring myself, therefore achieving none of the things that I set out to do for me. I wasn't a hero. I was totally gutless instead. Yet again, I was giving away my power to the energy vampires in my life.

In my defence, in the earlier chapters I did, in fact, hint about not fearing ghosts; our threat was of the living kind, and a quick brief mention about Joe, and I even threw in the chapter on forgiveness, which I said I might possibly have to revisit at a later stage. When was I going to do this? Did I not tell myself life is not a rehearsal; you do not get do-overs! It is now or never.

Thirty years of grief, stress, anxiety, and the trauma that my kids now both live with PTSD and anxiety was reduced to two small paragraphs. What is it that I am teaching my girls about their relationships and their true worth as a person?

If I am going to honour myself and get my voice back, it is going to have to be the full story, not sugar coated. This is what I was conditioned to do, protect the reputation of others by not exposing their reality and faults and their own mantra about how we don't display our dirty laundry in public.

As I type this, though, I have made a new self-discovery: I am not hurting anymore. I really don't care. I have let this go, I finally feel free, and I finally have the emotional strength to face what will be.

Joe, in my opinion, was loose cannon, easily upset, and would fly into a rage when anyone questioned him or disagreed with him and he was my husband's closest childhood friend. His main target was me. I must have been a threat to him in some way because I was always in his sights. Ironically I was always the only person who was honest with him while others just told him what he wanted to hear or smoothed things over as to not set him off or upset him.

In his rage, he took on a threatening persona. His eyes went black glazed and manic. If you have never seen this look, consider yourself lucky. The fear will never leave you. Unfortunately my kids and I would come to know this look well over the years. A relative of Joe's saw this look once and is still talking about how scared he was. Well, spare a thought for me and my kids if a grown man was terrified.

I would have to let this man into my home every night after work so he could visit because no one else wanted anything to do with him. While he was there, I would have to walk on eggshells so as not to offend him or start a conversation on a subject that he did not approve of, and that itself was a minefield. I am normally an open book and like to discuss a multitude of topics. This is where I began to lose my voice. Here I was in my own home and I had no rights. Even though I may have waited all month to watch something on TV, if I knew it would upset him and throw him into a rage, I didn't dare.

Did I mention how deeply religious this man was and how he crossed himself every night when he sat at the dinner table. This might have something to do with my lack of faith in the church or any such religious order. He also regularly visits with priests for counselling and considered himself pure of heart. While at the same time, he was exposing my children to endless mental and emotional abuse that was enabled by his family repeatedly and his few friends. I didn't care about what he put me through, but my kids were a different matter. They were off limits. Most people avoided him like the plague others feared him. His immediate family chose to continue to enable his bad behaviour just to keep the peace. Even my husband would make excuses making us the bad people and making Joe think that what he was doing was acceptable instead of calling him out on it.

The day he unleashed his tirade on my kids was the day something snapped in me.

In the Beginning, Life with Joe

After the birth of Mikaela, he started to change. At the age of 21, he was diagnosed with schizophrenia. The anger and attitude he would unleash on one of his relatives was now being redirected at me. One night, he dropped in for a visit. Mikaela was a few months old and unsettled. She wouldn't stop crying. I was home alone with him, as John hadn't returned from work yet.

I am not sure if she was crying because she was sensing my anxiety or because she was just a baby and that is what they do. They have their moments. After a while, he turned to me with those raging black eyes and told me to shove mineral turpentine up her backside to shut her up. I froze and took her into another room. It felt like hours before John came home from work.

After this incident, his psychiatrist asked to see me separately because I think he realised how much hatred Joe had towards me and the fact that I was in danger. He said if I was ever alone in my house with him and he lost it again, I was to run out of the house and keep running. I was to leave the baby and just run. Yeah, right! Joe hated me even more after this. He still brings it up occasionally from time to time that I had no right to speak to his psychiatrist, even though it was the psychiatrist who asked to speak to me.

After this incident, I was always afraid that he might try to tamper with my car. Every time I had to go out, I would drive around the block, test my brakes, and then return home to pick up my baby. On two separate occasions, my accelerator pedal got stuck. It was an old car. Luckily I wasn't a paranoid person. One of those times, John was driving. I don't think he would have risked John's life, but I always wondered if he'd done something to my car. I don't think he did, but it was always a real fear, and I wondered how far he would go.

We were never to talk about his condition or diagnosis, which started with S and ended with A. It would bring on another rage. If we do not talk about it, it did not happen.

Your home is your castle, or it should be—your haven, your sanctuary, a safe place to retreat and hide from the world. Mine became part of my nightmare and my prison.

All I wanted was to be loved and protected by the man in my life who was my world. I waited and waited, but loyalties were always split. At times, I hated my husband, and other times, I understood he was in a difficult position. I always felt there were three people in my relationship. At times, I wished there was another woman as my ticket out of there with my kids. It would have made things so much easier. John's loyalty to Joe was so strong and misguided it annoyed me. After all, I had a piece of paper that said he had to be there for me first.

Every night for years, my kids and I would have to endure Joe's visits. He would come into our home to watch TV and spend his time, as he had no other friends and I would have to be someone else so as not to upset him or provoke him.

It got to the point that at times when the kids and I were home alone, we would turn off the lights and close the blinds to make it look as if we were not home. Our home became our prison, and I would park my car halfway down a side street so he could not see it.

That was life. I could do no right. I had no rights. This was how I lived.

When Joe's sister Cathy was about to turn twenty-one, I offered to help organise her party, as she was in the middle of university exams and needed to study. I was at the venue with several of her friends who offered to help me to decorate and set up tables and chairs. As there was so much to do, I asked if Joe could do something for me instead of sitting there watching, as I needed all hands on deck if we were going to be set up in time. This was obviously the wrong thing to say, so he responded by picking up a butcher's knife and chasing me around the venue until someone else talked it out of his hand and sent him home to cool off. My heart still pounds at the memory, but I was meant to forget it and never mention it again. Another NDE but then again if I was to count all the ones at the hands of Joe, then my book will resemble a telephone directory.

A few days later, I confided in my mum. She was mortified. She called his mother to express her disgust at what had happened and then was doubly horrified by his mother's reaction. She found it amusing and laughed in a shrill laugh "As if he was going to kill her." My mother was speechless. How do you respond to that? Who lives like this and then questions why they get so sick?

When Mikaela was four and a half, she was sleeping in her bed and was woken by my screams just outside her bedroom door. I am so sorry for all the horrors this poor child had to witness, and I am so sorry that

I failed to protect her. She came out of her bedroom into a hallway to see her father trying to pull Joe's hands off my neck. No wonder I have lost my voice. It happens slowly and has nothing to do with your voice box. It took a brave woman like Jaycee telling her story, to give me the strength to speak up. The ghosts in my life were friendly, but this person constantly visiting our home was terrifying. I cannot to this day understand why I could not bring myself to take my children and leave.

My kids and I would have to be puppets as to not upset him or throw him into a rage. Over the years, there were thousands of instances with dramas, tantrums, and of course, they were always all my fault, because I was strong willed and stubborn and I always provoked him, according to his family. His family were enablers, and they always made excuses for his poor behaviour. He was a misogynist who thought women were placed on this earth to serve him.

On one occasion when he was trying to beat me while John was trying to pull him off me. I, in no uncertain terms, voiced my disgust to Joe's father that Joe has no right to hit me or touch me. Then another blow of how dysfunctional these people were was when Joe's father said to me that that was right—only my husband had the right to raise his hand to me, not Joe. Who were these people? What planet were they from?

As I had been running my own property development business for 11 years I had just attended an auction and bought another property. I was so excited. It was also funny how the agent got excited thinking he was going to have a bidding war after the young man in the sparkling Mercedes rolled up wearing a suit, bringing his bidders to three, or so he thought, as John didn't come and stand beside me. In the end, we were successful with the purchasing of the property and John went back to work while I went home.

Joe and Cathy dropped in shortly after for a coffee. While I sat with her at the kitchen table, he sat meters away in the sitting area in front of the TV. As I began telling her the story about how the auction had gone, he gave me the death glare and started screaming at me to shut up because I was too loud.

This time I lost it, and I asked him to leave. I told him that if he wanted to watch TV, he should have stayed at home. How dare he come into my home and tell me off with such aggression? Do you think I got any support from *anyone*? No, the consensus was, how dare I kick him out? Who did I think I was? I had no right to do such a thing.

John, instead of reprimanding him about his behaviour and supporting me, said to him, "You know how *she* gets." That still hurts. I had no rights in my home, and nobody to stand up for me. Whatever happened to those vows I had such respect for? Didn't I deserve respect? It was my home too. Wasn't my husband meant to defend me and protect me? Time and time again, I never mattered in my life or my relationship. I was never to come first.

Here I was in my own home without the right to kick someone out who was being rude and disrespectful to me, not to mention threatening. Instead of supporting me, my husband made me out to be in the wrong just to appease Joe's ego because he didn't want a confrontation. For this very reason, Joe was treated as a little boy and constantly enabled by those around him who smoothed things over by making excuses for him so as not to have to deal with his manic rants and rages.

Years later, Joe met and married Patsy. Yes, it is true—he found another mentally deranged human, whose hate for me surpassed his own. I was told later that for the first three months of their marriage she would rant and complain about me for at least three hours every night. Even that was supposedly my fault. I could do no right yet again.

Patsy was a woman who I had nothing in common with who I had nothing to say to and who, if anything, I avoided like the plague, because I knew she was loopy, for want of a better word. The marriage lasted seventeen months and produced a beautiful little girl who was innocent in all this.

Also during their marriage, I had to avoid talking about my property development projects because talking about my success would infuriate her further. So when Joe called my home late at night, and I was not home because I was on site, painting or working late, John would say I had book club with my friends, again trivialising what I did.

I often would have to listen to Joe's tirades as to how I was a kept woman. I was not permitted to say how I contributed to my family's income, and I was not permitted to set him straight. Joe never was to know that for the first eight years of our marriage I was the higher income earner in the relationship. Or that this is why I went back to work when Mikaela was six months old so I could pay the mortgage or that it was my redundancy pay out from a job that I loved that gave us the leg up to buy into a business that gave us the great life that we have now.

During Patsy and Joe's divorce proceedings, I had to appear in court as a witness because she accused me of stalking her by driving up and down her street with her ex-husband. I disliked both of them: Why on God's earth would I be wasting my day with him, driving around her house, which is a two-hour round trip from my home, just to catch a glimpse of her? Especially with all my other health issues that were also going on? She was not even remotely a priority in my life back then or ever. I then found out that she was stalking me. Go figure. People are so strange. I had no interest in them when they were married; I had even less interest in either one of them after their divorce.

I understand that they are both challenged people with mental issues, so I am not going to keep carrying this hurt around anymore, but surely, I should be permitted to speak out and say my story. I'm doing this for me and my girls, and I'm not interested in throwing anyone under the bus, if this embarrasses them in any way, maybe in the future they need to keep their behaviour in check and think about whether their actions are acceptable to the rest of the population. If it makes them uncomfortable, then perhaps it's not right or acceptable, and they perhaps should rethink what they put out.

Months after their separation, I took my kids over to visit while they had an access visit with Joe's infant child so the kids could see her and bond with her. She was a baby and very innocent. She loved spending time with my girls. I was determined not to let the child suffer because of her parents.

During this visit, the unthinkable happened. Up until now, all his anger and rage had been directed towards me. This time, he unleashed his anger on Ashley, who was nine years old at the time. I know you are dying to know what unforgivable act she committed against him, so I will tell you.

As she was sitting on the couch, her foot was touching his daughter's plastic toy. This sent him into a roaring rage. He hovered over her, abusing the proverbial hell out of her with that black, demonic death stare, all six feet two inches and 140 kilos of him. Then Mikaela yelled back at him. From then on, there was no stopping him. His father tried to stop him, his mother tried to stop him, but nobody could control him. If anything, in his rage, his daughter was in danger of getting tripped over while she was playing on the floor, by none other than him.

John was overseas on business when this happened, so I took control. This straw broke something in me. After all this time of me taking his verbal and emotional abuse time and time again, he made a lethal mistake by going after my kids. This was different, and it was not going to happen again. The kids and I ran out of the house fearing for our lives. We jumped in the car, drove around the block, and then and only then I stopped the car so we could buckle up. I had never been so scared in my life. We were all shaking like leaves.

After that, I tried to keep the kids busy. We were all far too shaken to go home, so we drove around for hours. When we finally did, there was no sleep for any of us that night. We all slept in my bed, and every time our dog barked, the kids thought it was him jumping the fence as he had done several times before. There was no consoling them. They were terrified.

At six the next morning, I got up, showered, and dressed, and by seven, I went back to his house to give him a tongue lashing that was years in the making. His parents were shocked to see me. They said he was still sleeping. Good to know he managed to catch up on his beauty sleep, because nobody in my house got any sleep that night.

When he came into the kitchen, I found my voice. After all the years of no voice, now I was a tigress protecting my cubs. I made sure he understood that the girls and I were dead to him. If he was to see us down the street, he was to keep walking and not approach us. He was no longer anything to us; he was a stranger. If he was to approach my front gate without an invitation, I was going to call the police and press charges. If he as much as upset my children by looking at them, I was going to ring his daughter's court-appointed lawyer and tell them my story; he would never have access to his child again. I was going to spill on the years of verbal, physical, and emotional abuse. I finally had this tyrant exactly where I wanted him.

In my rage, I then said words that I put out in the universe that I am not proud of. I said I do not know why god gave him and his idiot wife a child and I do not care if he throws his daughter off the Westgate Bridge; he was to leave my kids alone and not damage them any further. Then months later, a man threw his five-year-old daughter off that very bridge as payback to his ex-wife. He was also intending to throw his two boys over but was stopped by other motorists when they realised that a child was thrown over the bridge railing and not a doll, as they'd first thought.

To say I'd had enough of this verbal and emotional abuse over the years was an understatement. The anxiety and PTSD follows my kids to this day, and when I told him about how shaken they were, he laughed and offered them his medication. He had no remorse whatsoever; he thought it was all a big joke.

When John came back from overseas, I expected him to stand up and finally cut him out of our lives. After all the chances he was given, Joe just kept on stuffing up. They were all enablers and tried to smooth things over. None of them ever made him accountable for his actions or ever told him that his behaviour was unacceptable; it was always I that was at fault, and now it was my kids as well. I was the one always out of line, and I was provoking him, and it was totally fair enough that he would snap. "He just snapped." That statement was as if it made it understandable and acceptable repeatedly. I can't tell you how many times I heard that statement. Every time I did, I died a little more inside.

When I spoke to Cathy and told her that they were lucky that I put up with this behaviour for so long, because no other woman would be stupid enough to put up with the things that I had endured, her intelligent response was "You don't know that."

After years and years of my family hearing about the way the kids and I were treated, they began to lose respect for them. John has a hard time understanding why and why my parents and brother no longer attend functions at their home. To others, the reasons are obvious.

The other similarity between my life and the woman in the book was that if our tormentor had a good day, we sometimes had a good day. In our case, not always, because you were constantly waiting for the other shoe to drop; you were permanently on heightened alert. From that day, every time we drove down the street and saw him walking, our anxiety levels would escalate. Unfortunately, we were living in the same suburb, so he was a living, breathing, constant flashback walking our streets. Our code when we saw him would be a parody of another good old Australian song. We would say, "Horror movie right there on my windscreen, horror movie right there on my windscreen," and then our moods would just crash as we had to recall everything he represented to us.

My husband to this day forces the girls to call him on his birthday and wish him a happy birthday, when they'd rather wish him dead. It was yet another sense of betrayal for them. Poor kids, they were always left wanting their father's attention and approval. His approval was always conditional, provided they did right by Joe.

This is the grief and regret that tears you up inside, allowing illness to manifest and take over. For years, I'd go to the doctor and hope that he'd tell me I had a godawful disease so I could get out of my life, but there was no way I'd be leaving my kids in that house without me to offer them some sort of protection. See? Be careful what you wish for. Again, didn't I matter? What did my marriage certificate mean? I concluded that it meant absolutely nothing, so for a good ten years in quiet protest, I stopped wearing my wedding rings. Not that anyone else noticed.

When my eldest daughters twenty-first was approaching, I sent out the invitations and Joe was not invited, not that he ever knew this. Normally invitations are displayed on their fridge. This invitation was never displayed. Instead of making sure that he understood that there were consequences to his actions, he was asked to stay home and look after his father, who had just had surgery, to disguise the fact that he was not invited in the first place.

This is probably why forgiveness was so difficult and more like near impossible for me. How can you forgive when the person who has caused you and your children so much pain does not have any remorse or understanding that they have done wrong? I acknowledge that this dysfunctional family needs to go on its own journey and make amends for their own mistakes. Nothing annoys me more than parents who say things like "Say sorry, Johnny," and Johnny mimics a pathetic "Sorry," but doesn't mean it and, five minutes later, does exactly the same thing. Over the years, I've had thousands of these kinds of apologies.

He is now approaching his fifties. Seriously, his family needs to hold him accountable for his actions. Had he been taught the difference between right and wrong from a younger age, he just might have had a half-decent life. A complete life, with friends, a family, and a loving relationship. Then he could actually have been in a much happier place than where he is today. It's actually very sad.

As I said before, I don't wish him harm. I just wish him far from my family.

Every day I hear about the karma bus and how it has found them. It's funny that nothing seems to be going right for them. As I said, it is something they themselves have put in motion, and if they really truly are religious, they need to make peace with their God.

I feel for my husband, and I love him dearly. I acknowledge that this chapter is going to be very difficult for him because he has always known this culture where we do not tell and we cover up our messes. Now I just want to heal and move on. I am going to put myself first for a change. This is well overdue. This, unfortunately, like it or not, was part of my journey, and I am happy to say it has taught me many valuable life lessons.

This journey is just as much for John as it is for me. All I ever wanted was for him to put us first. If he had been firm with Joe when this all started and given him a clear ultimatum, I am, sure that Joe would not have risked his relationship with his best friend. By constantly making excuses for Joe, he has enabled him to continue this tirade on us, and I do not care about me, but Joe singlehandedly has destroyed my girl's childhoods and definitely limited them reaching their full potentials, not to mention giving them ongoing emotional issues they now have to live with daily.

Chapter 20

Betrayal

When I first met Cathy, she was not yet in high school, and she was constantly getting physically and emotionally abused by Joe. She would start to cry at the drop of a hat; she had no self-esteem, and I set to work to lift her up emotionally. She was the little sister I never had, so I protected her and stuck up for her.

She idolised my kids and they her. They had a special relationship. She was like not only a big sister to them but also a confidante.

In January 2015, she was telling everyone how she was taking Ashley and Joe's daughter, Jessica, on a dream holiday to America. Let's just say it ended up being a nightmare. Instead of showering them with love, she made sure she went out of her way to explain to my two girls that Joe's daughter was extra special to her, and that she was like a daughter to her, and that they just had to accept it. It was like their relationship status had changed overnight and my children just were demoted. My kids were left in shock wondering what they had done wrong.

On their first day on their holiday, she got up, dressed, and asked who was hungry. Ashley said she was starving. Cathy apologised to Ashley, saying, sorry, she had not paid for a breakfast for her. Therefore, Cathy left Ashley in the hotel room, took the younger girl Jessica for the buffet breakfast, and brought my daughter a plain bagel back to the room. Thank you very much. Is that how you care for a child that has been entrusted to you to take overseas to another country far from her home? I think not.

The verbal abuse and trauma continued. It was unrelenting. My girls were on the phone, constantly in tears. They couldn't understand why she had changed and why she was behaving like this. What had they done for her to hate them so much?

She would leave restaurants early and only pay for her and Jessica's meals, never allowing for tips or taxes, thus putting financial strain on all the others. All while she showered senseless and expensive gifts on the other child, often buying her stuff she did not even want. While splurging out of control on one child, she didn't even cover the food for the other.

What confused me the most was her spruiking to her friends and her family for months prior to the holiday about how she was taking the girls overseas and how much fun it was going to be? At no stage were we asked to cover Ashley's expenses, and she had asked her to bring only some spending money.

Looking back, I thank God that I never granted permission for her to take Ashley on safari in Africa a few years back when she had suggested it. I think she may have armed Ashley with a gun and sent her out to catch her own dinner. My interpretation of *I'm taking the girls on holiday* is very different. If it was me, what I'd do for one I would do for the other. But that's just me.

This was my life at that time. My kids were in America. They were calling texting and me in tears every day. Meanwhile, my mother was in ICU. She had just had a heart valve replaced and one repaired. She had to go back into theatre the next day to remove a blood clot from her heart, and a week later, she was still in ICU and critically ill.

My unfortunate thinking was that while I was taking care of my mum, at least my kids were in good hands, being loved and cared for by someone whom they adored. Instead, they were being betrayed yet again, and this was someone they had loved and trusted their whole lives.

Four months after her return, I invited her over to discuss what had happened. As a mother, and considering everything Joe had put us through, I had expected more from her. I believed that, in the past four months, I had calmed down enough not to rip her head off the minute she walked into the house. At the least I was willing to give her the opportunity to give me her side of the story. After all, it was only fair.

However, she walked into my home, sat down, and said, "I'm not here to discuss what happened. I'm only here to see how we can move forward." She repeated these words repeatedly, as though it were a rehearsed script, which infuriated me even more.

"Sorry, love, but before we can move forward, I need to know how you can take my child from my side and take her across the globe on the pretence that you will care for her. You did not feed her for three weeks, making my husband and I send over more than $2,000 spending money to cover her expenses and your tips and taxes that you failed to cover repeatedly. How is that you taking her for a holiday?

"Not only that, but you also demanded that they all go on tours that none of them wanted to go on. Hello! We could have taken her to Europe with us later that year. It would have been cheaper, less stressful, and more fun. Rather than the living nightmare, you put us all through. After all that, you seriously do not even think you owe me an explanation.

"You flat out told my children that they were no longer as important to you as Joe's child because you decided to take her on as the child you never had. Why couldn't you have said that to my kids while they were still here in Australia? You could have saved me a fortune on phone calls, text messages, stress, and trauma

"For God's sake, tell me you had a brain snap and a brain fart. I do not care. Give me something. You are human. I was willing to listen. Just do not give me this I'm-here-to-move-forward crap. You broke my girls' hearts, and you do not think I deserve an explanation? You are not a mum, and you just do not get it. Jaycee the woman in the book gets it!"

Shortly after this trip, Mikaela was diagnosed with multiple sclerosis, an autoimmune disease—again after trauma and emotion. The cycle continues.

Remember the Karma bus? Cathy's life has gone down the drain since she came home from that trip. She is always calling the girls, trying to mend fences, but words are words, and, well, sometimes it is hard to forget the words that cut so deep.

My girls are intelligent women. I would never tell them what to do. They are their own people and make their own choices and decisions. It is totally up to them what relationship, if any, they choose to have with her.

Cathy has now been diagnosed with her very own autoimmune disease and is struggling with the prescribed medication. Misery really does love company. I know it sounds like a rant but it really feels good letting it all out.

In March 2015, after the stress of my mum in hospital and this drama with my kids, my liver was crashing. My GGT was up at 944, and all the other liver markers were off the chart. My doctor was horrified.

With all that I had been through, was there any wonder why my autoimmune hepatitis was trying to kill me? This was where I decided that things were going to change, and my journey was going to take a turn. I was done trying to protect others constantly at the expense of myself and my kids, and enough was enough? Whoever wanted to follow me and be part of my new journey could hop on board. If not, I wished them well and onwards with their lives.

Joe and Patsy's mental illnesses had been part of my life and controlled my life whether I liked it or not. I should have the right to talk about it if I want to, without being silenced because it embarrassed others. If things cause you embarrassment, then you know deep down they are wrong and unacceptable. So stop this behaviour once and for all. We are all accountable for our actions and so are they.

I love my family, but right is right, and wrong is wrong, and wrong needed to be put right. I was no longer going to accept anything less. I suppose now I was strong enough to deal with it. Everything happens for a reason, and in divine timing.

I read through my book and realised the depth of my pain and all the anger that I had been carrying around inside me. I thought that *is one angry woman*. Well, no more, I was over it. A rant had been long overdue and bottled up for too long. They would have to pay for their mistakes, as we all do not to me, as I could no longer care less, but to their god.

I am healing, and I have come such a long way. Earlier, I said thank you for picking up my book, and I hoped that you would also find the inspiration and hope to achieve your dreams and live your life for you first, then others.

Now I thank that beautiful woman Jaycee for being so brave and helping me to stand up for myself and find my voice. I might never meet her in person, but she is an amazing woman and has inspired me. Thank you for sharing your story with me. If you had not, I would never have included these final chapters to my book, therefore not achieving any of the things that I was determined to do for myself. Therefore, it looks like my trip to Bali was constantly being delayed to correspond with the new release of this particular book. If you believe in divine timing, that is.

I do not wish harm on anyone, but everyone will get what is coming to him or her. It's just how it works.

I have always believed that things happen in threes. The murdered boy in Queensland, the rescued women from the American house of horrors, and the abducted child all have something in common and for some reason have become part of my journey. Maybe my life's purpose revolves around child abductions. Who knows?

Those who are embarrassed by my story obviously should have done things differently.

I also said earlier on that I am writing my book in the hope that it might help my kids and grandchildren in the future, if they end up with an autoimmune disease. The people who have caused all of this trauma and grief take no responsibility whatsoever, but that is OK with me.

I have let go of all that which no longer serves me. I no longer am a victim. I am a survivor, and I am definitely no longer renting space in my head or heart to people who do not deserve it.

Chapter 21

Along Came Amy

Earlier, I kept bringing up divine timing, and this is where my friend, Amy, comes into my life. Amy is a beautiful soul, wife, and mother of two. Amy's husband worked for a time with John, and they became good friends. She and I met very briefly many years ago at a work function and only spoke a few words, and that was it. It was just a greeting, to be perfectly honest.

A few years ago, they called John in as a friend and estate agent to sell their home. Amy, like me, is very intuitive, and although she tried to ignore it, she could not, and ended up buying me a voucher for three reconnective healing sessions. Quite a generous gesture, I might add, for someone she didn't even know.

She told me later that while she was talking to John she kept getting messages and was pestered until she carried out the message, just like the other psychics had said in the past. She was told to tell me that I do matter and that I am important too.

This is where the divine timing comes into it. The sessions are half an hour's drive from my home. The old Celeste would have not gone, end of story. However, the new Celeste understood that guides give us the information we require and it is up to us to listen.

After meeting Amy to thank her, I realised she was answering many of my questions, and I hers. Who could have known when we had met years ago how much in common we would have years later in terms of our spiritual development and journeys? I can't even begin to imagine my life without her now.

Reconnective Healing

Wow. Oh, wow! This is the only way to describe it. Amy's voucher led me to the amazing reconnection healer. For me, it has been a huge part of healing my heart, throat, and gut, and what an amazing journey it has been.

After my reconnection, I have dropped two dress sizes, and my bloating has gone away. My diet has not changed in any way, but the energy flow around my body definitely has, and this has in turn helped my body and digestive system to work more efficiently. The weight is now just dropping off. This after years of struggling to lose anything, whether I was dieting or not.

I carried all that pain and betrayal for thirty years, and the first thing that this healer said to me is, "You're not connected to yourself."

I was blocked in all my chakras. Not only that, but without me saying anything, she just validated everything I already knew about the fact that I was not being true to myself. Six sessions later, I am no longer bloated, my body is working better, and my energy flow is electric. I will also be doing the two final reconnection-healing sessions, and I cannot wait to see what changes that brings.

I am finally being true to myself for a change. I am also excited to walk through the next chapters of this journey together with the amazing people I have met.

I don't regret anything about my life, as my journey has made me who I am today. It has given me strength and attitude to get through anything. I will get up every morning and be grateful that I get to see the sky and kick ass because I am alive. If I can serve others, I will, and I hope to leave a positive footprint on this planet. But, most importantly, I'm also going to live for me and keep ticking those boxes.

While ticking those very boxes, I actually attended a psychic workshop held by a well-known Australian psychic.

Right at the beginning of the workshop, she told us that by the end of the day we would be doing readings from jewellery and photographs. I was petrified that I was way out of my depth and that by the end of the day everyone there would know I didn't have any gift and I shouldn't have been there.

No one was more surprised than me that from holding a photo I actually picked up all the ailments of the two people in the picture and that there was adoption in the family tree. There was a woman in the photo. I saw many children around her but didn't think that they were hers biologically. She had apparently adopted four of the man's five children. Now that is quite specific, and my accuracy was spot on. If only the messages were always as clear as they were that day.

The decades are passing, and my life is passing me by. I have decided I do not want to be an old person with regrets, so here it goes. I will be heard from now on. I do matter, and I am important too. I am alive because of sheer willpower and determination. I need to look in the rear-view mirror one last time just to be sure I finally leave the old me behind and start living my life again without all the baggage and secrets.

I need to be appreciated and respected as a human being. I am here to leave a positive footprint on this world and to make people laugh. There is far too much doom and gloom around already. I refuse to add anymore.

Well, there you go, warts and all; that is brutal honesty. I lost my voice. I lost my identity. From now on, I am not going to allow others to silence me.

This has been one hell of a journey. It is not unique by any means. I am sure many will identify with this, but we need to pull our rubbish out from under the carpet and sort it out like adults.

I am determined to write this book and put it out in the universe. Seeing as I have been guided thus far, I am going to allow the process to evolve as it is meant to. I finally feel like I have the strength to face this and to reclaim the kind of life I always wanted for myself but lost sight of over the years.

If my story is meant to help just one person find the energy to beat their illness and give them strength, then I could not be happier. It is a shame I wasted so much time and took so long to realise that I matter also, not just everyone around me. I can't believe that I had to get so sick to eliminate energy suckers from my life, had to almost die to allow myself to breathe again.

Now I understand that carrying around all that pain and hate for the people who caused my illness just gave them power over me. Therefore, after one last rant, I have now let it all go, but with a different mind-set. It will never happen again because I will not allow it. Things are very different now. I am a different person.

The other thing that I have learned on this journey is that everyone has a story; you just need to sit next to somebody and listen. I feel like I am viewing a wonderful world of ours for the first time. When you put this book down go outside and walk barefoot through the grass. Smell the roses and stop to talk to your neighbour for a bit. Reconnect with life and hug your family every day, as if it is going to be the last time.

Love and light xx

Printed in the United States
By Bookmasters